ES ANAGERS

(NG A SUCCESSFUL CV

SIMON HOWARD

DORLING KINDERSLEY
London • New York • Sydney • Moscow
www.dk.com

A DORLING KINDERSLEY BOOK
www.dk.com

Editors Gwen Edmonds, Corinne Asghar
Designers Laura Watson, Nigel Morris

Senior Editor Adèle Hayward
Senior Designer Tassy King

Managing Editors Stephanie Jackson, Jonathan Metcalf
Managing Art Editor Nigel Duffield

DTP Designer Jason Little
Production Controller Silvia La Greca

First published in Great Britain in 1999 by
Dorling Kindersley Limited,
9 Henrietta Street, London WC2E 8PS

This edition first published exclusively for
WH Smith in 1999

2 4 6 8 10 9 7 5 3

A CIP catalogue record for this book is available from the British Library

ISBN 0 7513 0885 4

Reproduced by Colourscan, Singapore
Printed in Hong Kong by Wing King Tong Co. Ltd.

CONTENTS

INTRODUCTION

The pace of change in today's world of work means that our CV is our passport to new opportunities, and consequently the most important career document we ever produce. There is no "right way" to create a perfect CV – we are all individuals and our CVs will all be different. Creating a Successful CV *guides you through planning, creating, and using your CV, and provides an introduction to psychometric testing. It will cause you to think about your attributes as a person, your skills as a professional, and your hopes for the future. Full of practical information and exercises, as well as over 100 invaluable tips and a directory of useful information for job-seekers, this book will help you to produce an effective CV and use it successfully.*

PLANNING YOUR CV

Your CV is a brochure, not an autobiography. Its purpose is to help you in the process of finding a new job by selling your skills and experience to the right person.

UNDERSTANDING CVs

Before you start compiling your CV, you need to familiarize yourself with the few basic rules of its construction. Everyone is different, and so are their CVs. However, the principles on which a good CV are founded remain the same.

1 Remember, a positive attitude about yourself is your greatest asset.

CULTURAL DIFFERENCES

There are many conventions about CVs around the world. In the US, a one-page CV is standard, while in continental Europe, many employers would expect a four- or five-page CV that includes detailed information on educational achievements and professional qualifications.

WHAT IS A CV?

Curriculum vitae (literally, "the course of one's life"), or "CV", is the term most commonly used in Europe. In the United States, résumé is the usual title. Its purpose is to provide sufficient information for prospective employers (or their agents) to register interest in you. There is more than one type of CV, and you need to decide which is the most appropriate for you. Your aim is to produce a CV that gets you to the next stage of the recruitment process: this may be an informal meeting or a telephone interview, or you may be sent an application form or called to a formal interview.

UNDERSTANDING THE PRINCIPAL TYPES OF CV

TYPE	USE
CHRONOLOGICAL Lists your employment history in reverse chronological order.	Most effective when you are applying for jobs in the same line of work and your CV demonstrates a clear record of career progression.
FUNCTIONAL Highlights your principal skills and strengths rather than career history.	Most useful for first-time job hunters and those seeking a change of career direction, as the emphasis is not on career history but on transferable skills.
ONE-PAGE SUMMARY Summarizes your career and displays your track record.	Most effective for senior managers or those looking for freelance or temporary work. May be specifically requested by headhunters or employers.

CREATING A "BROCHURE"

The principal role of your CV is to highlight your value to a potential employer, and to do that you have to promote yourself. A document that is just a career summary will not sell the attributes and skills you have to offer. So your CV needs to be a selling document – think of it as your career brochure. If you consider brochures you find appealing, they will be the ones that are well laid out, succinct, and easy to understand. Your CV should be exactly the same. If it is clearly presented and 100 per cent error free, this will say a lot about your motivation and focus.

▲ **GETTING AN INTERVIEW**
The usual purpose of your CV is to earn you an interview. If you are selected for the interview, it will probably be your CV that sets the agenda for that important initial meeting.

2 Set aside enough time to prepare and revise your CV – it cannot be done in just one evening.

SETTING OBJECTIVES

The more focused your objectives, the more successful your CV is likely to be. Identify those things that you have found fulfilling in order to help you be clear about future career goals, then analyze where you are now and where you want to go.

3 Remember, your career objectives will not be the same as others'.

4 Learn lessons from past experiences to use in the future.

LEARNING FROM YOUR EXPERIENCE ▼

Plot a simple chart to put your career in perspective – it will help to show you what to look for in a new job.

ANALYZING YOUR CAREER

Everyone has their own set of career expectations. For some, progress will mean upward progression to more senior roles. Others will be looking for their work to fit in with a particular lifestyle. Whatever your priorities are, your career will have consisted of a series of "career highs" and "career lows". Identify those highs and lows so that you can analyze your progress beyond the qualifications and experience you have gained.

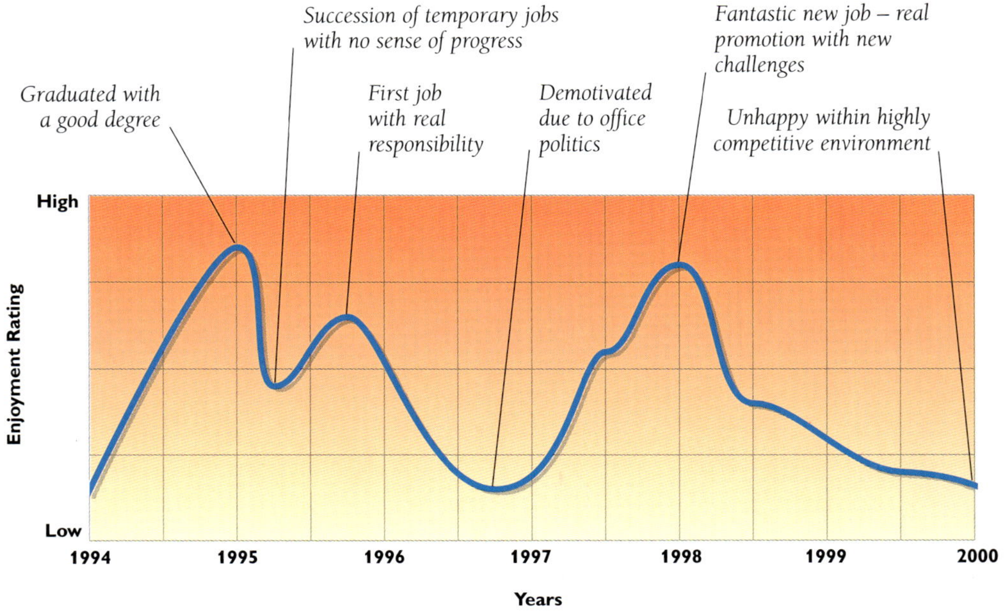

DECIDING ON PRIORITIES

Learning from the past is important for all career seekers. Your analysis of career highs and lows will help you to identify the features of your past experience that you will want to develop in a future career move. Some may be features that relate directly to the job, such as "to become head of department" or the location of the company. Others will be more subtle, such as "to feel comfortable with the team culture". Having identified these features, you must decide which are essential and which are desirable. Only you can decide on the priorities for your next move, but a clear list of objectives will help you judge any future job offers.

5 Be prepared to review and revise your objectives.

6 Be positive about what you can achieve in the future.

LISTING YOUR OBJECTIVES ▶

Only you can decide which of your objectives are essential – those elements a future job must have – and which are just desirable.

Be clear about what really is essential to you

Be aware that lifestyle considerations will change at different stages in your working life

ESSENTIAL

Job related: *Report to board level. Have control of project budgets. Run team of at least 8 people.*

Lifestyle: *Commute time of less than 30 minutes. No weekend travelling.*

DESIRABLE

Job related: *Be involved in new business development. Receive training in the latest technology.*

Lifestyle: *Be in walking distance of shops/cafes etc. Have some flexibility of working hours.*

7 Identify your long-term career objectives, and decide on your immediate aim.

DO'S AND DON'TS

- ✔ Do look at friends' and colleagues' CVs, if they are willing.
- ✔ Do be honest about aspects of work you do not enjoy.
- ✔ Do talk to others about their goals.
- ✘ Don't set unrealistic targets – you will be disappointed.
- ✘ Don't belittle your achievements or expertise.
- ✘ Don't set yourself negative objectives.

FINDING YOUR NEXT JOB

Before you set out on your job search, you need to be aware of the methods you can adopt for securing a job. There are four main routes – it is important that you do not rely too much on just one of them, but explore the potential of each route for you.

8 When possible, send your job application to a named person.

9 Always quote any reference numbers when replying to job advertisements.

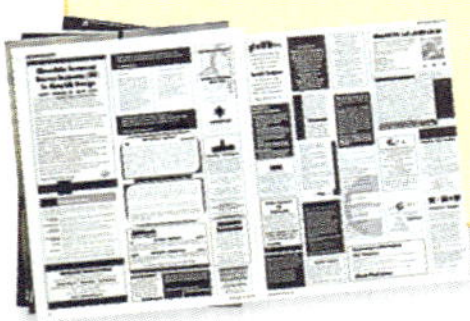

REPLYING TO JOB ADVERTISEMENTS

Employers and recruitment companies place many thousands of job advertisements every year. Through newspapers, professional magazines and journals, the Internet, and career fairs, applications are constantly sought. This is the most open and accessible market for jobs – and so the most competitive, but at least you know that employers who advertise are committed to recruiting.

CONTACTING RECRUITMENT COMPANIES

In general, recruitment companies find people for jobs, not jobs for people. Employers pay them a fee to provide qualified candidates, who can then be shortlisted for final selection. Although they rely on job seekers' CVs to make their money, the service they provide the job seeker varies enormously. There are two types of recruitment companies. The first type are those that operate databases, and these are often referred to as recruitment agencies. They range from the well-known high-street agencies through to firms specializing in professional or functional areas, such as finance or IT. Second, there are the search and selection companies who advertise or headhunt for individual posts. Both are important for the experienced job seeker.

THINGS TO DO

1. Make a note of which days the media advertise jobs relevant to you.
2. Search the Internet for useful recruitment and corporate sites.
3. Talk to colleagues about recruitment companies they can recommend.
4. Identify any trade events worth attending.
5. Monitor the press for companies that might be expanding.

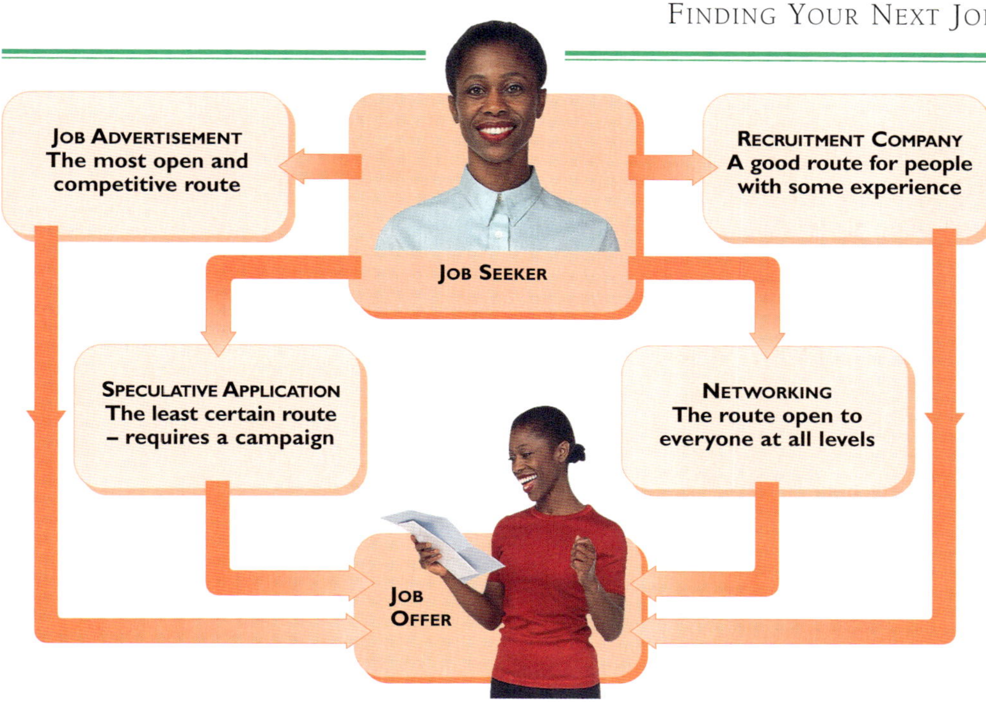

▲ **CONSIDERING ROUTES**
Whatever your current experience and ambitions, all four routes should be considered – any one could yield a job.

10 Be methodical – it may take months to find a new job.

MAKING SPECULATIVE APPLICATIONS

Personnel departments receive a steady stream of enquiries for what may only be a limited number of vacancies. However, if you have a clear idea of what you want to do and who you want to do it for, contacting employers directly can be effective. The key is to contact the right person with a clear proposition. Although a company may hold you on their database, keep monitoring job advertisements.

NETWORKING

Someone you know knows someone who is recruiting. "Network" – that is, communicate with your personal and business contacts – to find your next job. With this route, however, you must be proactive – to network successfully you need to tell people, discreetly, that you are looking for a job. It may be time-consuming, but for those starting out or returning to work, it can be very effective.

11 Let people know if they need to be discreet about your job search.

DECIDING ON YOUR STRATEGY

Unfortunately, when searching for a new job, you cannot simply produce one perfect CV. Every advertisement you reply to, every recruitment company and employer you approach, should receive an application tailor-made to their specific requirements.

12 Always consider who the likely reader of your CV is going to be.

CHOOSING THE RIGHT APPROACH

No two careers will be the same, so no two CVs will be the same, and no two career searches will be the same. It may be that you feel that there is more than one direction your career could take – you could choose to specialize in your own field or move into a more generalist managerial position. For the different routes you will need different strategies, focusing on different achievements and skills. Whatever your next step, assess the tactics most likely to be successful.

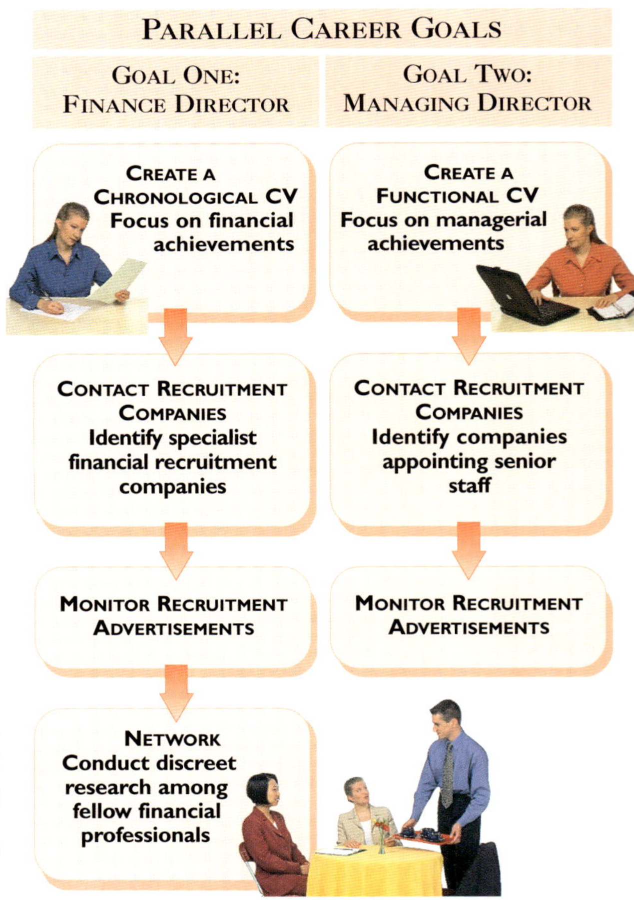

ADAPTING YOUR CV ▶
The two directions in which this financial director can see her career progressing require different CVs and approaches. Highlight different skills and experience according to the type of application.

TARGETING THE READER

Whichever strategy you choose to employ or route you take, an important consideration is the words you use – we all respond positively to people who "speak our language". Each audience has its own needs and priorities, so the content of your application needs to feed readers what they want to know. For example, try to feed back specific phrases used in job advertisements, highlighting how you fit those requirements. With every job application, keep your targeted reader in mind and create both your CV and covering letter with a view to their needs.

13 Avoid using too many specialist terms in your CV.

14 Make sure that you appear flexible to a potential employer.

15 Carefully consider temporary roles – they may get you the job you want.

DO'S AND DON'TS

- ✔ Do be selective about who you send your CV to.
- ✔ Do tell the reader what you want to do.
- ✔ Do ask the reader to respond.
- ✗ Don't send a CV without a letter.
- ✗ Don't dismiss leads and openings too quickly.
- ✗ Don't expect a recruiter to give you career advice.

BEING FLEXIBLE

It is not just through applying for permanent jobs that you might join a new employer. Increasingly, many people join an organization through taking on consultancy assignments or filling a temporary role. For all employers, flexibility is a key word, and so more temps, contractors, and consultants are employed than ever before. The same methods can be used as for finding permanent employment, but your proposition will need to be different.

You must also identify and target the correct person in either the employer or the recruitment company. With employers, contacting relevant line managers may be more productive than going through the personnel department.

CREATING OPTIONS ▶
By being flexible in your approach, you will create many new opportunities for yourself.

TARGETING YOUR CV

In order to make your CV as effective as possible, it helps to understand how it will be used by an employer or recruiter. Keep in mind that an employer will be looking beyond your skills and qualifications to ascertain if you will fit into their organization's culture.

16 Remember, recruiters are working for employers.

POINTS TO REMEMBER

- Readers will be looking for reasons to screen you out, so always reread your application.
- Your job application will be read by different people with varying perspectives and attitudes.
- Key words and phrases relating to the job need to be included in each application.
- A culture fit with a prospective employer is essential.

SELECTING YOURSELF IN

Unless you are very lucky, or possess incredibly scarce skills that are in demand, your CV will be one of many to land on the reader's desk. Among recruiters, it is a source of continuing debate as to whether they are trying to select candidates *in* by looking for positive indicators, or seeking to select them *out* by identifying reasons to reject them. In preparing your CV and covering letter, count on the reader doing both. It can be for very trivial reasons that applications are rejected at the paper sifting stage; the secret is to plan for this and to try to get inside the mind of the reader.

MAKING YOUR CV SCANNER-FRIENDLY

Your CV may not be read by human eyes. Some larger employers and recruitment companies will scan your CV into their recruitment systems. Their software then identifies key words and phrases in your CV and matches these with the requirements of a role. These systems may be used whether you submit a hard copy or e-mail a text file. In order to make your CV scanner-friendly, first make a list of the key words and phrases that cover both your skills and experience and then interweave them into your CV. Second, ensure that the layout is clear and has no unusual typefaces.

17 Keep copies of any applications you e-mail.

18 Avoid companies you know have bad employment records.

MAKING THE RIGHT MOVE

As this case illustrates, the working environment of an organization is as important as the job itself. Be honest with yourself about the type of company culture that you will find challenging and enjoyable.

CASE STUDY

After gaining her English degree, Laura worked in a small publishing house for three years, where she was promoted twice. Shortly after her 25th birthday, she joined a larger international publisher where she hoped to gain broader experience and work overseas. Everyone congratulated her on making a good career move: bigger job, more money, larger company, more opportunity. However, she left after only nine months. The job was a good one, and she did it well, but the greater formality of the company – the layers of management, the memo writing, and lack of social life with any of her colleagues – was not her style. When she applied for her next job, this time with a smaller company, she was careful to match the probable company culture with her own desire to work in a smaller, less structured, and more friendly environment.

LOOKING FOR A MATCH

Employers and recruiters are trying to identify a match between you, the job you are applying for, and the organization's culture. This is the basis of all good employment relationships, and as a result you are more likely to become a committed and motivated employee. When screening your CV, the reader will not only be looking for evidence of your capability to do the job, but also trying to judge whether you are the sort of person who will be compatible with the organization.

19 Think hard about the working environment that will suit you.

FINDING A MATCH

Aim to find a job match that balances the needs of your employer, your skills and experience, and your own personal needs.

The style and behaviour of the organization is easy for you to fit into. You respond positively to the working environment

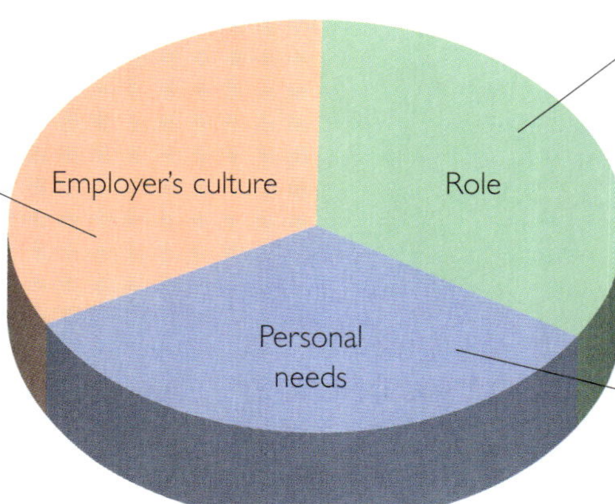

The requirements of the role match your skills and experience. You can do the job today and are positive about where it might lead in future

Your skills, personality, and experience match the culture of the organization and the needs of the role

UNDERSTANDING TRANSFERABLE SKILLS

Your qualifications and experience are only part of your personal assets. Your behaviour as an individual is more important to employers than what you know, and they are more interested in what you can do in the future than what you have done in the past.

20 Be clear about your strengths so that you are able to communicate them.

QUESTIONS TO ASK YOURSELF

Q Which skills lie behind the work I enjoy doing?

Q Do I use skills in my personal life that people do not see at work?

Q Who can I ask to give me an objective opinion about my transferable skills?

Q Which skills do I want to develop and use again?

IDENTIFYING SKILLS

Transferable skills, core skills, soft skills, personal attributes, competences – these are all terms used to describe broadly the same thing: the underlying aspects of you as an individual that indicate how suited you will be to a particular role. They relate to your behaviour, personality, values, and motives, as well as to your skills and experience. By looking at the chart opposite, you will recognize that you possess some of the skills listed, but you will also have skills that are not so readily identified, and it is important that your CV is able to pinpoint these.

LOOKING FOR EVIDENCE

A CV is a highly subjective document. It is based on your own assessment of yourself. However, the more objective your CV can become, the more powerful it will be. Anyone can claim to possess excellence in all the transferable skills listed opposite, but they will not be believed. However, if you can demonstrate evidence of possessing transferable skills through your past achievements, you will appear credible in your claim. Remember to always back up your claims with the hard evidence of results.

21 Demonstrate your skills through events in your past.

22 Add to your CV any non-work skills that you possess.

TRANSFERABLE SKILLS

MANAGERIAL QUALITIES

- **LEADERSHIP**
  Motivates others to reach team goals.
- **PLANNING AND ORGANIZING**
  Organizes and schedules events, activities, and resources. Monitors timescales and plans.
- **QUALITY ORIENTATION**
  Ensures quality standards are met.
- **PERSUASIVENESS**
  Influences and convinces others leading to acceptance, agreement, or behaviour change.

PROFESSIONAL QUALITIES

- **SPECIALIST KNOWLEDGE**
  Understands technical or professional aspects of work, and updates knowledge.
- **PROBLEM-SOLVING AND ANALYSIS**
  Analyzes issues and makes systematic and rational judgments based on information.
- **ORAL COMMUNICATION**
  Speaks fluently to individuals and groups.
- **WRITTEN COMMUNICATION**
  Writes in a clear, concise, relevant manner.

ENTREPRENEURIAL QUALITIES

- **COMMERCIAL AWARENESS**
  Understands commercial principles. Views issues in terms of costs, profits, and added value.
- **CREATIVITY AND INNOVATION**
  Creates new and imaginative approaches, and questions traditional assumptions.
- **ACTION ORIENTATION**
  Makes decisions, takes initiative, and originates action.
- **STRATEGIC THINKING**
  Demonstrates a broad-based view of issues.

PERSONAL QUALITIES

- **INTERPERSONAL SENSITIVITY**
  Interacts with others in a sensitive and effective way.
- **FLEXIBILITY**
  Adapts to changing demands and conditions.
- **RESILIENCE**
  Maintains effective behaviour in the face of setbacks or pressure.
- **PERSONAL MOTIVATION**
  Shows enthusiasm for goals and career commitment.

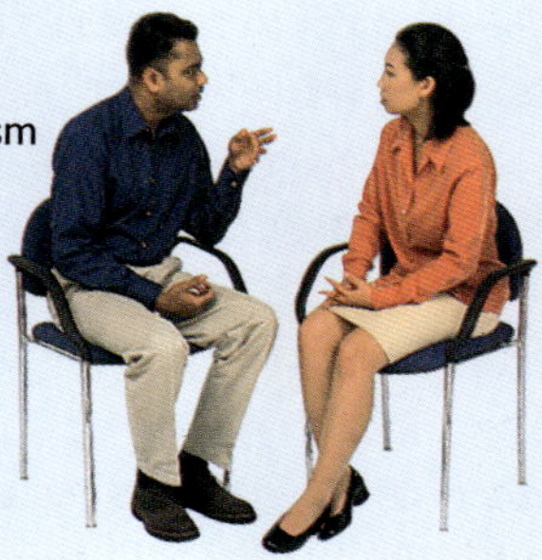

IDENTIFYING YOUR TRANSFERABLE SKILLS

The instructions that follow will help you to carry out a mini-audit on your career that will identify your transferable skills. However, it is not enough to simply pinpoint your skills – you also need to think about how much you enjoyed using them.

23 Try to secure work you enjoy to ensure you find job satisfaction.

THINGS TO DO

1. Write a brief outline of your career to date for quick and easy reference.
2. Keep all the notes you have made about your skills and objectives.
3. Keep ready to hand a copy of your present job description to refer to.

LISTING ACHIEVEMENTS

First, identify a minimum of ten achievements of which you are proud. They may come from your personal or work life – the balance will depend on your circumstances. Think creatively about what you might count as achievements – they are not just the obvious things. In your personal life, you may hold a position of responsibility that calls for the use of skills you do not normally use at work. You could also have had to deal with events that may not have been particularly enjoyable, but have nevertheless demonstrated capacities and talents you may not have realized you possess.

RECOGNIZING SKILLS

To identify your skills, break each achievement down into its component parts. Think about what each component part was and which skills you used. Using a chart such as the one opposite, score the frequency with which you used a transferable skill – you may be surprised by the results. (Refer to the list on p.17 for detailed definitions.) Be aware of the skills you use in your personal life – some people find that their personal lives display a wider range of skills than they use at work.

24 Be honest when analyzing your skills – try not to be modest or arrogant.

DRAWING UP YOUR SKILLS CHART

- List ten achievements
- ↓
- Identify the skills you used
- ↓
- Rate your enjoyment level and your wish to re-use skills
- ↓
- Discuss your assessment with a colleague
- ↓
- Review your results

SCORING AND CHECKING

Now rate on a scale of 1–5, where 1 is low and 5 is high, how much you enjoyed using each particular skill and then the degree to which you want to use it again. Being proficient at something and enjoying doing it are not always the same thing. Finally, take a reality check – this is not easy. Choose someone who knows you well and talk them through your analysis to come up with an overall reality rating for each skill.

> **25** Talk to friends and colleagues about what they identify as your strengths and weaknesses.

ASSESS RESULTS

Skills you can demonstrate and that you enjoy and want to use again are obvious priorities. Skills that you rate enjoyable and want to use again, but can only demonstrate limited evidence of, are clearly areas for career development. Keep the results of this mini-audit to help in preparing your CV and covering letters – they are the key words, phrases, events, and ideas to include in all your applications.

	Frequency	Enjoyment	Reuse	Reality
Managerial Qualities				
Leadership	3	4	4	3
Planning and Organizing	2	3	4	2
Quality Orientation				
Persuasiveness				
Professional Qualities				
Specialist Knowledge				
Problem-Solving and Analysis				
Oral Communication				
Written Communication				
Entrepreneurial Qualities				
Commercial Awareness				
Creativity and Innovation				
Action Orientation				
Strategic Thinking				
Personal Qualities				
Interpersonal Sensitivity				
Flexibility				
Resilience				
Personal Motivation				

Give a score of 1–5 for each of your skills in every category

Assess a number of skills relevant to your personal life

FOCUSING ON STRENGTHS ▶

A chart such as this one may seem time-consuming to produce, but it will prove an invaluable tool in your job search.

CREATING YOUR CV

The content of your CV needs to be prepared with meticulous attention to detail. Set aside plenty of time to write, edit, and design the layout for maximum effect.

PREPARING THE CONTENT

Your CV and letter are often the first contact you have with a prospective employer, and may receive just 30 seconds of their time on first reading. Ensure that your CV contains the right information in the right order in a form that is easy to read.

26 Avoid using overly formal language in your CV or covering letter.

27 Ensure that your CV is concise and easy to read.

28 You have complete control over what to include and exclude in your CV.

CREATING A GOOD FIRST IMPRESSION

Every part of your application must be an invitation to read more. A succinct and relevant covering letter will encourage the reader to turn to the CV. A concise front page will encourage the reader to look beyond just your qualifications and current position. Remember, these initial, vital impressions have to achieve one thing: to ensure that your application is put on the "possible" pile. Decide whether a functional or chronological CV is more appropriate for your application – the reader must know straightaway why you can do the job.

Use good-quality paper and a clear, pleasing layout	Shows that you are business-like and organized
Write in an easily readable style, with good use of English	Shows that you have good communication and writing skills
Communicate complicated subjects simply and clearly	Shows that you are a concise thinker
Make sure that there are no spelling mistakes	Shows that you have good attention to detail
Select relevant personal information and career details	Shows that you have good judgment
Include appropriate qualifications and employment history	Shows that you are qualified to do the job

◀ **CONVEYING A MESSAGE**

The 30 seconds that an experienced recruiter may spend looking at your CV will tell them much about you as a prospective candidate. Everything, from the type of information you include, through to the paper and envelopes you choose, says something about you.

DECIDING ON LENGTH

Unless the one-page summary is being used, how long should your CV be? The general rule in the UK is preferably two, but exceptionally three, pages. In two pages you will be able to provide a convincing record of your recent achievements, outline your relevant experience and qualifications, and give the reader sufficient personal information to make the decision that you are worth seeing. If you are required to list technical skills or publications, then a third page may be acceptable. Be rigorous about editing out anything that is not relevant.

RANKING INFORMATION

You are writing your CV for the reader, not for yourself. It is down to you to judge the importance of different types of information through the reader's eyes; your educational achievements may be impressive, but if these are not a top priority to the reader, leave them until later. As the reader progresses through your CV, there must be a clear and distinct order that moves from essential information to additional information.

29 Ensure that your abilities are not obscured by too much detail.

DESCRIBING YOURSELF

You may use only 100 words to describe yourself in your CV, but the impression these few words leave and the conclusions readers draw from them are critical. As with every other aspect of preparing a CV, you must plan this with precision.

30 Put degree letters after your name only if they are really relevant.

31 Make sure that your voice-mail message is clear and business-like in case potential employers call.

DEVELOPING A PERSONAL STYLE

It is not just what you say, it is the way that you say it. Too many job applicants resort to an old-fashioned, overly formal style of writing in their CV construction and letter writing. In some cases, this even extends to writing the CV in the third person. In everything you write, adopt a plain-speaking, jargon-free style that allows the content to shine through.

BEING YOURSELF

Your name is the first line of your CV. But before you start, remember the one golden rule of CV construction: you are creating a document of which you will be proud to say, "This is me". So, if you are Mike Bagshaw in your work life be Mike Bagshaw on your CV. Do not become Michael Bagshaw, or G. Michael Bagshaw, or Gordon MICHAEL Bagshaw, or G. M. Bagshaw, or Gordon M. Bagshaw, unless that is actually your "trading identity". If you have professional qualifications or accreditations, decide whether to include these after your name. The general rule is, if they are relevant to your application they should be included. However, if they are not relevant, or are bought memberships, then they are best avoided altogether in your CV.

QUESTIONS TO ASK YOURSELF

Q Reading through my CV, am I happy that it sounds like me?

Q Do I want to be contacted at work or will this jeopardize my current position?

Q Is my CV written in plain English that a non-specialist could understand?

Q Is there any personal information that is particularly relevant to my application?

Q Does my selection of personal information and interests give an impression that I am happy with and can justify?

GIVING CONTACT INFORMATION

You must make it as easy as possible for interested readers to contact you. Clearly your full address is essential, although if you spend significant periods away, highlight this fact and offer an alternative means of contact. Include as many telephone contact points as you can – a work number if you can take calls there and a mobile number if you have one. E-mail is increasingly used, so include a personal e-mail address if you have regular access to one.

32 Include your nationality only if it will help your application.

▼ PROVIDING CONTACT INFORMATION

The contact information you give should be clear. An employer or recruiter will not want to try to get hold of you on several different numbers. Make sure you check for messages regularly.

Ensure your name is clear and easy to read

Include your full post code – it shows attention to detail

Neil Thomas
48 Cherry Tree Drive
Winslow
Beds BE12 6BV

Tel/Fax: 02044 304 4598
Mobile: 01797 395878
E-mail: Nthomas@brinter.com

Use your home rather than work e-mail address

OWNING UP TO AGE

In the US, information about your age should not be included, but in the UK it is seen as a relevant piece of information. The reader will guess at your age from other dates in your CV, so there is no point in leaving it out. The rule to follow is, if you believe your age is significant to your application, include it on the first page. Otherwise, list it under "other personal information".

CULTURAL DIFFERENCES

Every country in the world has its own conventions about what is and is not included in a CV. The US has the strictest laws governing what an employer is entitled to know about you as an individual. In continental Europe it is more usual to include a photograph with an application, particularly in Germany and the Benelux countries, and detailed descriptions of schooling and higher education are also usually required. On occasions in Japan and the Far East, only graduates of certain universities may apply to particular employers.

33 **Ensure that you reveal only positive information about yourself in the CV.**

POINTS TO REMEMBER

- Too many time-consuming interests may suggest you have little time for work.
- Your interests may be open to negative interpretation.
- Employers will only be interested in your home life in as far as it has an impact on your working life.
- Employers will draw conclusions about the type of person you are from your interests.
- Any personal successes or achievements outside the work place should be highlighted.

GIVING DETAILS OF YOUR HOME LIFE

Conventions vary from country to country, but whether you are single, married, separated, or divorced, this is one aspect of your CV that is hard to get right. Sometimes – for example, when the job involves travel – it may appear positive to be single. However, if the job requires someone who is settled and secure, a married person may seem more suitable. In fact, neither presumption is at all correct. If you choose to include your marital and family status, be aware of two things: first, ask yourself what conclusions someone screening your CV might draw from your statements. Second, decide whether you believe it is relevant to the application you are making. If it is, and you choose to include it, it is best put on the last page.

34 **Remember that you may be asked about anything and everything you have included in your CV.**

CASE STUDY

Terry and his wife lived in Perth, Scotland, but were brought up in the east of England and were keen to return after the birth of their two daughters. His family sent the jobs pages from their local newspapers, and he started applying for jobs. Although a well-qualified engineer, Terry was getting nowhere with the jobs he applied for. A friend in human resources looked at his CV and told him to make one small change. Where he had put "married, 2 children" he should add "keen to relocate to home area". His friend explained that, faced with many suitable applicants, an employer may be put off by the prospect of a candidate whose family would have to resettle to a new area and meet the costs of relocation. In a 30-second skim-read of his CV, the Perth address and "married, 2 children" were working against him.

◀ **CLARIFYING INFORMATION**
As with this case, make it clear, in both your CV and covering letter, why your application should be taken seriously. If there are issues such as relocation or extensive travelling, reassure employers that you are happy about the prospect. Avoid putting yourself in the position of being rejected through a misunderstanding of your circumstances.

EMPHASIZING INTERESTS

What you do in your spare time can say a great deal about you. So you must be aware that in selecting which interests you include, you are painting a picture of yourself for the reader. Rock climbing or walking suggest an active person, while pursuits such as archaeology or reading indicate that you have an enquiring mind. A penchant for DIY may show that you are practical, while painting or music suggests creativity. If you take part in charity work, the reader may infer that you are socially conscious, while youth work or chairing voluntary bodies may show your leadership potential. Sports can suggest either a competitive individual, or a team player.

▲ **COMPLETING THE PICTURE**
Your interests give you an opportunity to tell an employer a little more about yourself than simply your work achievements to date. Try to make the information relevant and emphasize the useful skills that you have mastered in pursuit of your interests.

35 Try to sound as objective as possible.

36 Avoid the use of "I" – it is implied throughout.

BEING AWARE OF BIAS

All good recruitment is about discrimination – discrimination in favour of the more able candidate. However, you must also count on some of the readers of your CV succumbing to less constructive bias. Like it or not, presumptions will be made from whatever personal information you include on your CV. By combining elements of that information, it is possible for readers to draw unethical and inappropriate conclusions about gender, race, and sexual orientation. So be careful not to provide too much information that could be negatively misconstrued.

SUMMARIZING EDUCATION AND TRAINING

The achievements you gain through education and training represent both acquired knowledge and your ability to develop. Many employers spend a lot of money on training and are looking to see if you are a person they should invest in.

37 Highlight any training undertaken through your own initiative.

DESCRIBING EDUCATION

There is one simple guideline here. The more recent your education, the more complete the description needs to be. At age 23 your educational record will form an important part of your achievements, and will be of significant interest to an employer. However, at age 43 your employment history counts for far more and your education is, for the most part, of only passing interest. For both educational attainment and professional qualifications, the guideline is that the more relevant and more recent they are to your application, the more complete the description and the earlier they should appear in your CV. Less relevant and less recent qualifications should be left to the last page. This is your first opportunity to highlight your achievements, so consider heading this section "Qualifications Gained" or "Educational Achievements", thereby introducing a positive vocabulary.

38 Leave out any exams or courses in which you have been unsuccessful.

▼ **KEEPING UP TO DATE**
There are many courses available that you can use to update your skills. Initiating your own training shows you are motivated.

OUTLINING PERSONAL AND CAREER DEVELOPMENT

If you have a formal professional qualification, the details of this need to be included with your education history. However, unless critical to a particular job application, details of other training do not generally merit a first page appearance. Consider heading a section on the second page "professional and personal development". Under this you could include formal training as well as initiatives you have undertaken that do not carry a certificate but are important to your career development.

▼ TRAINING RECORD

If you have an impressive record of training courses attended, mention the topics and dates – but limit it to those that are recent and relevant.

39 List your academic achievements and career history to date in reverse chronological order.

DO'S AND DON'TS

- ✔ Do consider the relevance of your academic record to an employer.
- ✔ Do include any special citations in exams or courses, if relevant.
- ✔ Do regularly update your IT skills.
- ✔ Do make this section of your CV positive.
- ✘ Don't include bought qualifications.
- ✘ Don't include subjects in which you are weak, such as a foreign language.
- ✘ Don't include training that has no bearing on an application.
- ✘ Don't go into unnecessary detail.

AVOIDING OVERLOAD

Be careful not to let your skills and experience be lost in a CV that contains much irrelevant information. Space in your CV is precious, and the following can generally be omitted (unless specifically requested or particularly relevant to your application): health, religion, driving licence details, national insurance number, nationality, passport number, place of birth, next of kin, political affiliation, failed exams or courses, names and ages of your children.

SELLING YOUR EXPERIENCE

Having described yourself and your qualifications, you now have to convince an employer that you have the right experience and attitude. It is important that the language of this part of your CV is positive, jargon-free, and concise.

40 Read your CV to a friend – it is useful when checking for clarity and fluency.

THINGS TO DO

1. Check each sentence carefully, word by word, and delete any unnecessary or irrelevant words.
2. Make a list of words appropriate to your job and skills.
3. Take time to find alternative words and phrases to avoid being repetitious.

USING THE RIGHT WORDS

Creating a positive first impression depends on your vocabulary and tone, as well as the facts that you are putting across. For the most part, your CV looks at your career in retrospect, so you should use the past tense. However, when describing current challenges, the present tense sounds more active. Never use "I" and avoid "me" or "my" – they can appear boastful and over-confident when you are trying to make your CV appear an objective appraisal of your abilities. Look at the list of action words opposite and focus your mind on the type of words that should appear in your CV. Compile a list that is specific to you.

USING POSITIVE LANGUAGE

It is vital that you write your CV and covering letters with confidence. There is no better way of displaying that confidence to prospective employers than by using positive language to describe positive situations. Here are some examples of how to improve phrases:

"*Met project timescale*"
becomes
"*Achieved project timescale*"

"*Responsible for repair programme*"
becomes
"*Headed induction programme*"

"*Implemented quality procedures*"
becomes
"*Drove quality programme*"

"*Suggested product enhancements*"
becomes
"*Devised product improvements*"

41 Draw on all your experience in drafting your CV, and then edit it down.

USING A CAREER SUMMARY

The reader of your CV should be able to pick out your skills and achievements instantly – most experienced recruiters will not take much notice of a career summary. There are, however, two instances where a summary may be useful: first, if you are writing to an individual inexperienced in reading CVs. Second, a career summary may help in a functional CV in which your employment history does not clearly show your skills.

KEEPING IT CRISP

Short sentences are read and understood. Longer sentences incorporating too many ideas will lose the reader. CVs that are written entirely in prose are difficult to scan quickly, but CVs that are endless lists and bullet points can be boring and characterless. You need to strike a balance.

42 Start all bullet points with a positive word or statement.

INCORPORATING ACTION WORDS

USING INITIATIVE	SOLVING PROBLEMS	MANAGING SITUATIONS	ACHIEVING TARGETS
Bought	Advised	Appointed	Accomplished
Built	Analyzed	Appraised	Achieved
Created	Combined	Approved	Completed
Designed	Cut	Controlled	Conducted
Engineered	Examined	Developed	Delivered
Forecast	Identified	Directed	Demonstrated
Formed	Investigated	Drove	Exceeded
Generated	Reduced	Employed	Improved
Improvised	Reorganized	Guided	Increased
Initiated	Resolved	Headed	Obtained
Instigated	Revised	Inspired	Produced
Launched	Solved	Led	Promoted
Originated	Streamlined	Managed	Secured
Pioneered	Trimmed	Ran	Selected

DESCRIBING YOUR EXPERIENCE

A straightforward description of what you have done and who you did it for is not enough. The reader must be able to see your record of achievements, and so appreciate what you will be able to do in the future for his or her organization.

43 Do not waste space on your CV listing employers' full addresses.

ACHIEVEMENTS AND RESPONSIBILITIES

The most common complaint about many CVs is that they are no more than a series of potted job descriptions. What an employer needs to know is how well you did what you did. Your present job description may be a useful place to start, but it was prepared for another purpose. Your CV needs to get you another job, and what you say about your responsibilities and achievements is critical.

POINTS TO REMEMBER

- An employer is looking for ability even more than experience – it points to the future.
- Specialist terms are only appropriate if you are sure the reader will understand them.
- The culture and ethos of your present organization may be of interest to a future employer.

44 Avoid exaggerating results, however important they are.

DEFINING SUCCESS

All successes on your CV must have features that are quantified and supported by outcomes. For example, "Led team of software developers" could be quantified to: "Led a team of 6 software developers on a £2m, 12-month project". There must also be an outcome – "Led a team of 6 software developers on a £2m, 12-month project. Achieved target time-scale. Project gave 30 per cent productivity gains for program users".

▼ **SHOWING OUTCOMES**
An event is of no significance without an outcome. Between the event and the outcome, add some quantifying detail.

DETAILING EMPLOYERS

You cannot assume that the reader will be familiar with the employers on your CV. Even if you work for a well-known company, the department you work or worked for will not be known in detail. You need to describe briefly the core activity of the employer and add some detail to it. This could include sales turnover, number of employees, profits – whatever relates most to your line of work. You may also hint at the "corporate health" of the organization at that time: was it thriving or undergoing a period of major change? This will help the reader put your experience in context.

EXECUTIVE OFFICE

◀ **DESCRIBING JOBS**

Two people with similar job descriptions may have very different work experiences. Employers like to know in which type of environment you are used to working.

OPEN-PLAN OFFICE ENVIRONMENT

45 Be confident and business-like when describing your achievements.

46 Use numerals – they are quicker and easier to read than words.

USING JOB TITLES

Both the content of your job and the job title itself will need some clarification. The meaning of a job title may vary from one organization to another, so use a generic job title if you can. It is better to write "Manager – International Assignments" than "International Assignment Manager". You will also need to summarize your responsibilities. One way of doing this is through a short, one- or two-sentence précis, or use a heading such as "accountabilities" or "responsibilities". Finally, avoid using too much space to state the obvious, but make sure you include any interesting, unique, or unusual aspects of your role.

QUOTING DATES

Readers do not like gaps, and yet many people's careers will have them. You need to demonstrate a record of progression, but you do not need to account for every month of your life, so stick to years when giving employment dates. If you have had more than one job with the same employer, use one overall heading for the employer, with joining and leaving dates, and then treat each role as a subheading – giving dates for each. If you are currently not in work, do not suggest you are, as your employment status will become apparent.

48 Ensure your CV spans your whole career, though you do not always need to go into details.

47 Put all the most important information on the left of your CV.

QUESTIONS TO ASK YOURSELF

Q Have I covered all periods of employment?

Q Have I included too many irrelevant details about earlier jobs?

Q Have I been consistent in my use of headings and bulleted points?

Q Is the language of my CV positive without sounding overbearing?

USING BULLET POINTS AND NUMBERS

A bullet point (as shown) or number is an invitation to the eye to "read this" and helps the reader to scan your CV.

- Start each bullet point with a positive action word.
- Avoid starting a bullet point with a qualification, such as, "As part of project team..." or a passive statement, like, "Participated as a member...".
- Where the nature of your experience makes it appropriate to do so, group your achievements under numbered paragraphs, each of which has a number of specific features.

GROUPING JOBS TOGETHER

At some points in your life, you may have worked in quick succession in a number of jobs. If these were with the same employer, try to group these together under generic headings and emphasize the range of experience gained. However, it must be clear to the reader that the high number of roles does not indicate that you were moved around or could not settle in any particular post. If the jobs were with different employers, were they permanent roles or was it a series of temporary engagements? Too much movement in the recent past can give a negative message.

DESCRIBING TEMPORARY JOBS

Many people use temporary employment as a means to an end at different stages of their careers. At the outset, this may have been to fund a university education, or gain work experience. Later, it could be a vehicle for returning to work, or as a stop-gap between permanent jobs. Do not feel obliged to describe each of these assignments in detail. A prospective employer will be more interested in the initiative and commitment you have shown in taking temporary work. It may also give you the opportunity to highlight a diverse range of experiences gained through a variety of different assignments and working environments.

▼ **RANKING INFORMATION**

A prospective employer giving your CV a 30-second scan needs to be able to see who you worked for, what your job title was, and what you achieved.

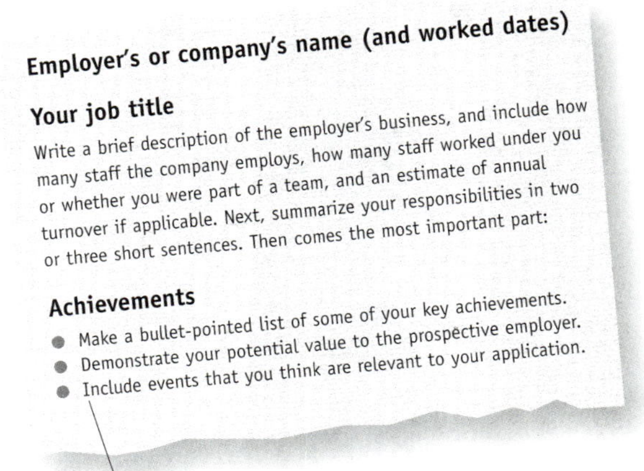
Employer's or company's name (and worked dates)

Your job title

Write a brief description of the employer's business, and include how many staff the company employs, how many staff worked under you or whether you were part of a team, and an estimate of annual turnover if applicable. Next, summarize your responsibilities in two or three short sentences. Then comes the most important part:

Achievements

- Make a bullet-pointed list of some of your key achievements.
- Demonstrate your potential value to the prospective employer.
- Include events that you think are relevant to your application.

Items highlighted by bullet points will be picked out by an employer scanning your CV

DESCRIBING PREVIOUS WORK

As you progress through your CV, the descriptions of previous employment should become shorter. It is only relatively recent jobs that require a full description of your achievements and responsibilities. While you may be very proud of what you achieved in a job ten or more years ago, this is unlikely to be of interest to the reader. Indeed, if your early employment is irrelevant to your current application, do not attempt to explain it at all; give only dates and the name of the employer.

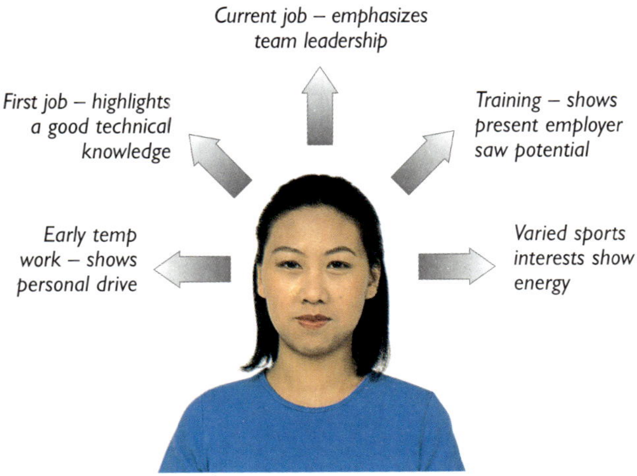

▲ **BEING SELECTIVE**

You can demonstrate to a potential employer that you have good judgment by the information you include in your CV. You need to select relevant experiences and then go on to highlight the reasons for their relevance to your application.

DECIDING ON LOOK

There is no right way to lay out your CV, but there are plenty of things to avoid. Visual layout is probably the most subjective aspect of your preparation, but the objective is clear – to ensure that your CV is user-friendly and easy for the reader to scan.

49 Look at other people's CVs for layout and presentation ideas.

POINTS TO REMEMBER

- A simple layout, without too many levels of heading or styles of type, is the most effective.
- It is impossible to underestimate the importance of a well-presented and pleasing CV.
- Legibility is your aim – you are not looking for a design award.

SELECTING A TYPEFACE

Keep it simple – you will not score any points for using fancy typefaces. What is more, if you e-mail your CV, you cannot guarantee the recipient's PC will be set up for non-standard typefaces. If your CV is to be electronically scanned, the simpler the typeface the better.

50 Consider creating a style of CV suited to e-mail.

STRUCTURING YOUR CV'S LAYOUT

There are essentially three core elements to your CV. Each element must be easily recognizable to the reader as a distinct section.

- Contact and personal information that is important enough to appear on the first page.
- Relevant employment history.
- Additional relevant personal information.

Times Roman — *A classic, elegant face gives an impression of maturity*

Times Roman Italic — *Italic may be hard to scan*

Times Roman Bold — *Bold type is good for picking out headings and dates*

Helvetica

Helvetica light — *A sans serif face is extremely easy to read*

Helvetica Italic

▲ COMMON TYPEFACES

The choice of a typeface is subjective, and the only important criterion is that it is easy to read. If it is one of the commonly used faces, it will be more easily scanned electronically. Only use one typeface throughout your CV. Even if you are applying for a job in a design-based field, do not let the design hide the message.

Large headings waste space and are unnecessary

16pt maximum for headings

12pt for body text

10pt for body text

Avoid making the main text too small

▲ **SETTING LEVELS**
Use different type sizes for different levels of information. Make sure that you are consistent and that headings of the same importance are the same size.

CHOOSING THE TYPE SIZE

Using too large a point size will waste valuable space, too small and the text can appear dense and difficult to read. Your CV is a business document, so follow the usual practices for such correspondence. As a guide, use 10–12 point for the body text and nothing over 16 point for headings. Restrained use of bold text and capital letters will also help the reader pick out key facts.

51 Avoid using coloured type – it may look good but it does not scan, photocopy, or e-mail well.

CHOOSING PAPER AND ENVELOPES

Use A4-size paper in white or near white, of good quality, and photocopier friendly. When choosing paper, think about the state your CV will be received in – too thin and it will look tatty, too thick and it will be permanently creased. When posting your CV, fold it only once and use an appropriately sized envelope.

Remember that your CV will be seen and handled by many people, so the quality of the paper and envelopes you use is very important

USING TEMPLATES

Many word processing packages will include standard templates for CVs. These can take some of the hard work out of the task of CV preparation and so are worth considering. However, be careful that the system does not prompt you to include unnecessary information or waste too much space. And remember, standard packages are just that – standard and ordinary – yet your CV needs to be both unique and extraordinary.

CUSTOMIZING TEMPLATES ▶
Use a computer template to help with the layout, not the content of your CV.

GETTING IT RIGHT

Your CV is almost complete. Having spent so much time preparing content and layout, now comes the quality control stage. It is important to check your CV thoroughly for mistakes; get a friend to give it a final read.

52 Use spell-checkers, but be aware that they will not find all mistakes.

POINTS TO REMEMBER

- All information that is specifically requested should be included.
- Employers want to know how well you did what you did, not just what you did.
- If asked to include salary details, always include any important perks and bonuses.
- Useful feedback given by friends, recruiters, employers, and colleagues should be acted on.
- Achievements and transferable skills are the key interest points in your CV for an employer.

53 If asked for a photograph, send a good quality one.

54 Include references only if specifically asked to do so.

THINGS TO AVOID

- **Do not lie:**
  It is accepted that your CV will be a positive statement of your career to date. However, there is a clear line between favourable presentation and blatant misrepresentation. Do not claim you have attained qualifications you have not, attended courses you have not, or worked in roles you have not. If you are found out, your employer would be entitled to cancel your employment contract, since you misled them.
- **Do not include salary details:**
  As with most good brochures, the price list should be published separately. At this stage, the reader is assessing your suitability, so your remuneration is not relevant. However, you may be asked to provide current salary details, and/or a record of salary progression. This should be done in the covering letter.
- **Do not attach a photograph:**
  By preparing your CV, you have carefully constructed a document that leads the reader to form a positive and objective opinion of you. The inclusion of a photograph may tempt a recruiter to make subjective decisions based on your appearance. However, the fashion or hospitality industries may request photographs, in which case you should include one.

GETTING A SECOND OPINION

Choosing someone to read your CV is not easy, so it makes sense to ask someone who understands the work you do. More often than not, people are too diffident in what they write about themselves, so you may be encouraged to be more bullish. Listen to the responses you get and then decide what changes will improve your CV.

Interviewee responds confidently to questions

Interviewer refers frequently to CV

▲ **APPEARING CONFIDENT**

It is essential that you can expand on and justify everything in your CV. Approach an interview with the same positive attitude you have brought to your CV and letter writing.

DO'S AND DON'TS

- ✔ Do check spelling, punctuation, and your use of tenses.
- ✔ Do use action words and positive phrases in both letters and CVs.
- ✔ Do adjust your CV to different situations.
- ✘ Don't undersell yourself.
- ✘ Don't forget the importance of first impressions.
- ✘ Don't include references – they will be requested later.

55 If requested, include salary details in the covering letter.

PREPARING FOR INTERVIEWS

When your CV has done its job and you are called for an interview with an employer or a recruiter, it is your CV that will probably set the agenda for that meeting. Often the recruiter will know nothing more about you than is contained in your CV. It is at this point that the quality of your CV will become clear and any inconsistencies, flaws, or misunderstandings will come to light. Be prepared for any awkward questions you think may be raised, and think about the answers you will give so that you can reinforce the positive impression given by your CV.

56 Read your CV again before going for an interview.

ADAPTING YOUR CV

The example CVs in this chapter show how different styles are appropriate at different times. Understanding these styles will enable you to produce the most effective CV.

TAILORING YOUR CV

Think of your CV as a living document – in fact, not just one document but many. Your life never stands still, so neither should your CV. Just as different people see different sides of you at different times, your CV should change according to the situation.

57 Be prepared to edit, re-edit, and revise your CV many times.

QUESTIONS TO ASK YOURSELF

Q Am I looking for a change of direction in my career?

Q Have I made a list of my transferable skills and career objectives that I can refer to?

Q Do I understand the difference between a functional and chronological style of CV, and when to use each one?

Q Do my skills and experience match the jobs that I am applying for?

CHOOSING THE RIGHT CV

Too many people write their first CV and then spend the rest of their career modifying the same document. But at different times of your life you will need different CVs. At some points in your career you will be selling your potential; at others, your employment history. However, it will always be your transferable skills that ultimately win you the job. Look at each of the example CVs in this chapter to see if there are elements that are relevant to you. Remember, whatever skills you are seeking to communicate in your CV must be supported by evidence of their use.

BEING AWARE ▶

As this case illustrates, the one overriding factor that influences the content and structure of your CV is the job you are applying for. It is the person who is going to read your CV, and what it is they are looking for, that should dictate how you put your CV together.

CASE STUDY

Steve had worked for seven years in an advertising agency, rising to the position of group leader. However, he now felt that the pressure of constant deadlines and frequent late nights were eating into his quality of life. In applying for jobs outside advertising, he at first used a conventional chronological CV, but was advised that, for an employer outside the advertising sector, the job titles and companies he had worked for offered little insight to his abilities. After auditing his career, he identified his transferable skills and used a functional CV, focusing on his skills in task management, training, team leadership, and attention to detail. Almost immediately, his conversion rate of "applications sent" to "calls for interview" improved. He now works in a team leadership role in the financial services industry.

CHANGING APPROACH

No two employers and no two jobs are identical, so no-one leaves one job to fulfil exactly the same role for another employer. It therefore follows that in your job search one CV will not fit all situations. Whether it is a matter of slightly modifying your CV for a specific job application, or writing a completely new CV, you should change your approach to meet the needs of each situation. This is particularly true if you are applying for jobs outside your own employment sector – here you are selling your potential to do well in a particular job, rather than selling your history of having done well in other jobs. You must also be prepared to skillfully tailor your CV for a particular application in order to highlight the precise skills and range of experience you know an employer is looking for.

58 Remember, an employer wants to see your potential.

THINGS TO DO

1. Read all relevant job advertisements.
2. Pick out the relevant skills and experience that each job application requires.
3. Consider connecting to e-mail and the Internet if you think they will help.
4. Review your career objectives regularly, and carefully adapt them.
5. Ask a friend to read and comment on your draft CV.

59 Make sure that, whatever job you are applying for, your skills and achievements stand out.

APPLYING FOR YOUR FIRST JOB

At this stage, your CV needs to show your potential – that you are somebody worth investing in. Employers may respond to your CV by sending you an application form. Approach the form as you have your CV, focusing on your achievements and skills.

60 Be creative in your approach to your CV, but follow the basic rules.

FIRST JOB: FUNCTIONAL CV

Start with full details of your educational record

↓

Summarize your relevant achievements

↓

Include a career objective if decided

↓

Describe any relevant work experience and skills

61 Remember, employers look for enthusiasm and motivation.

ORDERING INFORMATION

When looking for your first job, the best format for your CV is the functional one. You need to list full details of your education – these will be your main achievements to date. Think hard about your other accomplishments – you will need to identify them from your academic, working, and personal life. They will then need to be described in a way that will make them appealing to an employer. If you know your career objective, include this on the first page. Follow with brief details of any work experience, and if you have other skills, such as IT, round these up in a section entitled "Business Skills".

DO'S AND DON'TS

- ✔ Do identify the key achievements that are relevant to your application.
- ✔ Do include details of education courses and examination results.
- ✔ Do include a relevant career objective.
- ✗ Don't include unnecessary details about temporary jobs.
- ✗ Don't be unrealistic in your aims.
- ✗ Don't waste space – it is perfectly acceptable for your CV to fit on to one page.

STRESSING POTENTIAL ▼

A first CV needs to list all academic achievements but, unless they are exceptional, your CV will not stand out. To make your document distinctive, you need to concentrate on your skills and experience beyond your education.

> **62** If you are exploring more than one career path, create more than one CV.

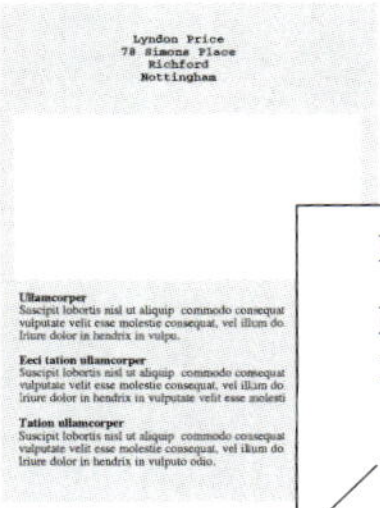

FIRST PAGE

This information may be helpful to an employer

Date of Birth: 12 March 1977 UK National

EDUCATION

1988–1995 Riverside High School, Newcastle.

1993 10 GCSEs at C grade or above (English and Maths at A grade)

1995 3 A Levels: Maths (B), Economics (B), French (C)

1996–1999 University of York

BSc Economics 2:2 Modules included:

Elements of Economics	State and Society
Economics Methods	Economic History
The British Economy	European Economics

ACHIEVEMENTS

- Chair of Finance; University Rag Committee 1997/8
- Elected Student Union representative
- Represented University and School in athletics
- Self-funded Gap Year, including 8-month trans-European trek
- Vacation work experience to gain IT skills
- School prefect

CAREER OBJECTIVE

To obtain a graduate trainee role in which I will be able to train for CIMA or ACA in order to progress in a generalist management role

Details of exam grades should be included, but omit exams that you have failed

A variety of experiences shows initiative

If known, a career objective should be stated with each application

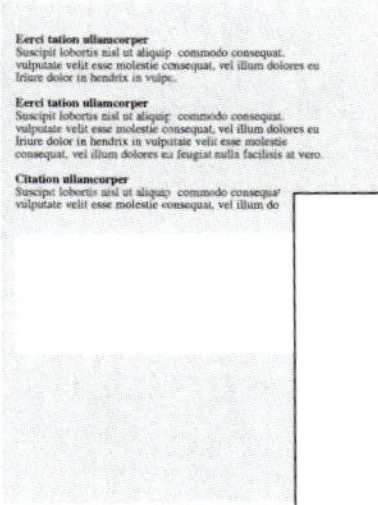

LAST PAGE

IT skills are so important that any experience or training is worth featuring

BUSINESS SKILLS

- Regular Internet user
- PC owner with a full range of spreadsheet and word-processing skills
- Customer service experience in retail and hospitality temporary roles
- Full driving licence

LANGUAGES: Fluent French

REFERENCES: Available on request

Languages are useful only if highly developed

MAKING YOUR FIRST CAREER CHANGE

The work experience you have gained in your first job should equip you with the confidence to make a positive career move. You are also more likely to have a clear idea of what you want from your career and your next job.

63 Aim high, but be realistic about what your next move should be.

FIRST CAREER CHANGE: CHRONOLOGICAL CV

Start with a brief summary of your educational record

↓

Describe your current job, highlighting your achievements

↓

Summarize other employment and include skills

↓

Finish with other relevant personal information

ORDERING INFORMATION

Use the chronological format to produce the strongest CV if your career move is within the same field. Your education is still recent enough to be of critical interest to an employer, so begin with a brief account. It is important to assess exactly what you have learnt from your work experience and to emphasize your achievements – this is now the core of your CV. Your career objectives will not appear on your CV, but it is worth spending time clarifying what they are.

CAREER OBJECTIVES

64 Always appear positive about your working experiences.

▼ PRIORITIZING INFORMATION

The emphasis of your CV has moved from your personal life achievements to your career achievements, although any relevant personal accomplishments still deserve a mention.

John Headley
13 Brookford Drive
Upper Longford
Kent

FIRST PAGE

Age 25 Marital Status: Single. Prepared to relocate.

EDUCATION

Secondary: 10 GCSEs 3 A levels: English (A) History (A) Geography (C)

Higher: University of Exeter: BA English & American Studies, 2:1
Graduated 1996

With less than five years' experience, education is still important

CAREER ACHIEVEMENTS

International Model Factors **1997–date**

IMF imports a wide range of automotive and aircraft models for the toy and connoisseur markets. Products are sold to the trade and through a direct marketing division. Current turnover is £22m, with 320 employees at Perth head office.

Assistant Product Manager **1998–date**

Responsible for the "Heritage" range of automotive models. Working closely with design department, involved in all aspects of product planning, sourcing, and trade marketing.

Achievements

- New range currently exceeding sales targets by 20%
- Ensured product range was launched on time within the promotional budget
- Planned and executed trade marketing programme, working closely with the advertising agency.
- Completed initial feasibility study, Board approval gained for range extension
- Identified and negotiated agreement with new supplier in China

This is a positive statement of achievements, backed up by evidence

Management trainee **1997–1998**

Initial assignment to Human Resources team in Salisbury, followed by an intensive training period at the company's training centre.

It is not necessary to go into detail about all training undertaken

LAST PAGE

Many employers look positively on a gap year

Gap year **1996–1997**

Travelled through Asia and the United States. Worked in restaurants and customer call centre in Denver in order to partly fund the trip.

Various temporary roles **1993–1996**

During the first 2 years at university, worked in a variety of part-time and vacation roles to support funding of higher education. Gained experience in customer service centres, reception work, and office administration.

The fact that work was undertaken is probably more important than the nature of the work itself

OTHER PERSONAL INFORMATION

Interests: squash, reading (particularly 20th-century history), trail walking, music (piano), keeping up with university friends.

University activities: captained University 2nd Squash team. Directed music for University revue. Chair of Debating Society.

CHANGING JOBS MID-CAREER

With at least ten years' experience behind you, your CV has become your most important career document. It must reflect all the commitment you have made to your career and the achievements that now make you marketable.

65 Do not include reasons for leaving a job in your CV.

MID-CAREER CHANGE: CHRONOLOGICAL CV

Start with a detailed account of your current employment

↓

Give a full list of all your significant achievements

↓

Summarize your previous employment and roles

↓

End with any other relevant personal or educational details

ORDERING INFORMATION

Unless you are considering a complete change of career, the chronological form of CV is definitely the preferred format. An accurate description of past and current responsibilities together with your record of achievements is critical – what you do now, and have done in the past, are the key elements of your document. Details of your education are less important – relevant education and qualifications should appear, but after your employment record. Remember the "more relevant, more recent" rule. Summarize earlier employment, and give full details of your recent professional development.

66 Make the most of all the professional and social contacts you have.

QUESTIONS TO ASK YOURSELF

- **Q** What methods should I use to find a new job?
- **Q** Who can I talk to off-the-record about my next move?
- **Q** Am I clear about my priorities, both career and lifestyle?
- **Q** When would be the best time to start applying for a job?
- **Q** How soon do I want to leave my current employment?
- **Q** Am I prepared to relocate – in this country or abroad?

SHOWING RESULTS ▼

At this level a future employer wants proof of your effectiveness – a certain amount of statistics help to make your CV appear more business-like.

67 Use the past tense in your CV, for example "managed" not "managing" – it will read better.

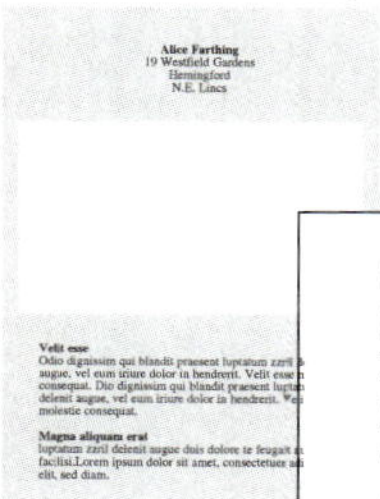

FIRST PAGE

Some explanation of an employer's activites is helpful, and figures give substance

CAREER SUMMARY

Electron Group International (EGI) **1996 – present**
Human Resources Director, Europe.

EGI designs and manufactures semiconductor processing and measurement equipment. The European Division has 5 principal development/manufacturing sites (UK, France, Germany, Italy, Eire) and a further 8 sales/service locations. 1999 European sales Euro364m, European employees 3,800.

A very brief job description is all that is needed

Responsible at Divisional Board level for all HR activities. Pan-European team of 65 HR professionals based in 9 locations.

Achievements

- Established HR team from scratch in 4 locations
- Negotiated pan-European pay & benefits review
- Recruited 22 senior managers across all management functions
- Restructured HR team and functional responsibilities
- Led Divisional project team investigating new manufacturing location
- Resolved EU training grant dispute

Although brief, these points cover a range of activities

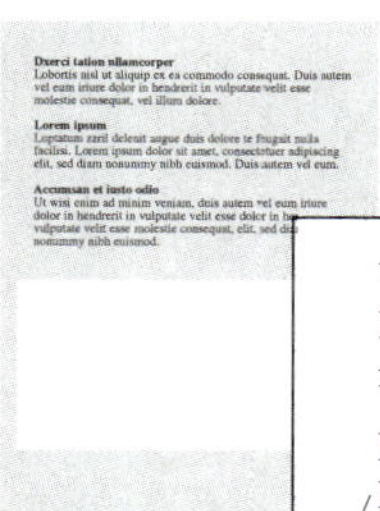

LAST PAGE

This is included to account for a time which would otherwise look like an unexplained gap

Various temporary roles **1977–1979**

Prior to taking a graduate trainee-ship, worked in a variety of temporary roles in the UK and Europe.

EDUCATION & PROFESSIONAL QUALIFICATIONS

Fellow of Institute of Personnel Development (FIPD)	1989
University of Sussex: BSc (Hons) Engineering	1977
Truro School: 3 A levels, 8 O levels	1966–1974

Relevant professional qualifications head the list

PROFESSIONAL DEVELOPMENT

HR leadership short course	INSEAD	1997
Assessment Centre Technology	Roffey Park	1991
Counselling skills at work	CEPEC	1989
Accredited to use aptitude & psychometric materials	Saville & Holdsworth	1985

PERSONAL INFORMATION

Languages: German – fluent, Italian – business level
Age: 44 (DOB 18/8/55)

CV compiled 18/9/99, all information correct at this date

This is useful as there may be a delay before an interview takes place

LOOKING FOR A CHANGE OF DIRECTION

There was a time when a job was for life; this is no longer the case. You may change your career direction for any one of a number of reasons. Whatever the reason, you need to present your experience in a way that is attractive to those outside your sector.

68 See a new start as an opportunity to make the most of skills you enjoy.

CHANGE OF DIRECTION: FUNCTIONAL CV

Start by highlighting your transferable skills

↓

Include your career objective if you have one

↓

Give a summary of your relevant employment history

↓

List relevant and recent education and courses

BRANCHING OUT ▼
Moving into a new field can be difficult, be clear in your own mind of your worth to a prospective employer.

ORDERING INFORMATION

Too many people seeking a change of career direction will use a chronological CV format. This means that the potential employer must try and distil from a range of previous experience (which at first glance is not apparently relevant) the skills in which they may be interested. Much better that you use a functional CV format that highlights your skills and supports these with your employment history. It is therefore critical that you have audited your career and identified your core skills; be certain that those skills you are emphasizing will be attractive to an employer. If you have decided on a clear career objective, consider including it.

69 Highlight different core skills, depending on the nature of your application.

Identify your core skills → **State your career objectives** → **Tell an employer what you can do**

SOUNDING POSITIVE ▼

Emphasize your key skills – your actual career history can be dealt with quite briefly. Ensure that your covering letter sounds positive about your previous work experiences and keen for new challenges.

70 Make sure that you are seen to be making a career change for all the right reasons.

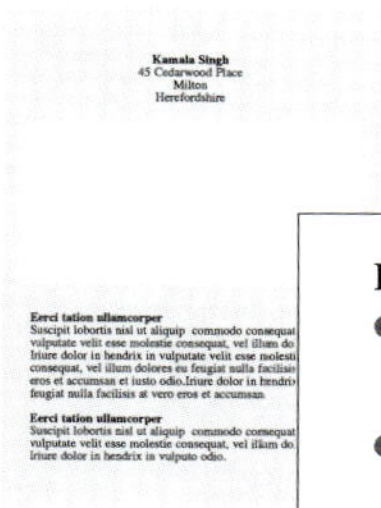
Kamala Singh
45 Cedarwood Place
Milton
Herefordshire

Eerci tation ullamcorper

Eerci tation ullamcorper

FIRST PAGE

Skills cover those used in a number of different roles

A positive word sets the tone for each description

Objective is focused, but not too specific

KEY SKILLS

- **Team leadership:** Led teams of 10–22 people on-site and in the field. Keen interest in training and coaching. Strong record of team achievement.
- **Project management:** Managed relocation of entire customer support centre. Headed review of support centre operations, subsequently implementing report recommendations.
- **Customer orientation:** Pioneered strategic relationship management programme with key customers. Strong rapport with customer managers.
- **Organizing:** Implemented support centre customer satisfaction and response time measurement systems. High level of attention to detail.

CAREER OBJECTIVE

To use key skills in a broader customer support management role, gaining experience outside computer-service sector.

CAREER HISTORY

Fry Systems Ltd – Service Centre Manager **1991–1999**

- Led team of 22 help desk support engineers
- Responsible for all field service personnel

The career history will echo some of the elements of the list of key skills

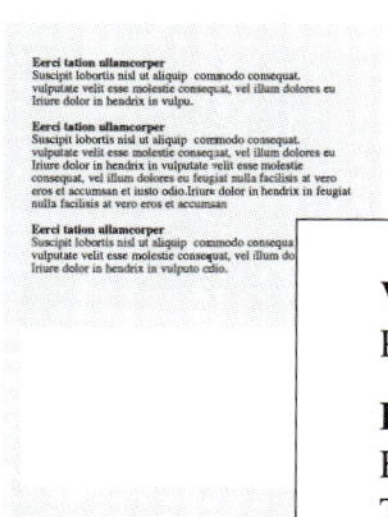
Eerci tation ullamcorper

Eerci tation ullamcorper

Eerci tation ullamcorper

LAST PAGE

Apply reverse chronology to all lists of courses

Various Temporary Jobs 1981–1982

Prior to taking a sandwich course, worked in variety of temporary roles.

EDUCATION

Esher College: BTEC Electronic Engineering 1984

Thames Ditton High School: 2 A levels, 7 GCEs 1973–1981

RELEVANT COURSES ATTENDED

CETEC – Customer relationship management 1997

Timespan – Effective time management 1995

Lakes Centre for Team Leadership – Advanced course 1991

PERSONAL INFORMATION

Married, 2 children.

Age: 38 (DOB 11/11/60)

RETURNING TO WORK

As when you were first looking for a job, your main aim now is to convince an employer that you are worth investing in. You must show what you achieved before your break, and that you are motivated and eager to brush up on any rusty skills.

71 Make a point of learning IT skills at every possible opportunity.

RETURNING TO WORK: FUNCTIONAL CV

Start with a profile of your experience and goals

↓

List the transferable skills acquired during your career

↓

Give details of your education and qualifications

↓

Finally, list your achievements and relevant experience

ORDERING INFORMATION

After a break from work, it is unlikely that a chronological CV will serve your purposes – you need to use a functional CV to emphasize your skills and achievements. A short profile of yourself will help an employer see your worth. The skills that caused you to be successful before you took your career break were your transferable skills, and are just as relevant now as they were then. What may be a little out of date is your knowledge – your knowledge of the sector or your learned skills, such as IT. An employer needs to see your record of achievement before your break, and be convinced of your motivation.

72 Only you can judge a job against your lifestyle criteria.

SETTING PARAMETERS ▶
Be clear about how your working life needs to fit in with your personal life. However, do not spell it out in an application – you could appear to be inflexible.

REASSESSING YOUR CAREER GOALS

Be selective about what you include in your CV – account for your whole career and any breaks, but give details only if they will enhance your CV.

73 Show that you are motivated by undertaking training while you are preparing to return to work.

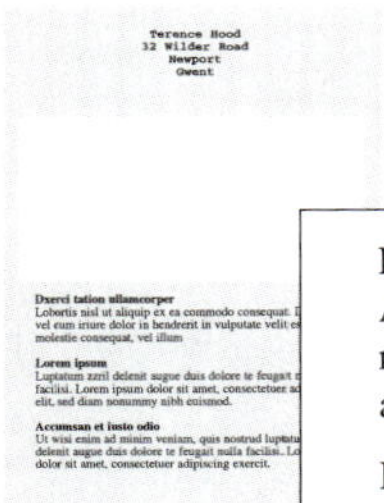

FIRST PAGE

This profile incorporates both a statement of career history and present objectives

PROFILE
Accomplished bilingual (French/English) Management Accountant with experience in the retail, distribution, and financial-services sectors, wishing to pursue a career in accounting and financial analysis.

KEY SKILLS

- Identifying management information needs and developing strategies to ensure user-friendly and precise reporting of financial performance.
- Ensuring accurate and timely reporting of financial performance at division and head office level. Experience of units with turnover of £2m to £100m.
- Designing and developing communication programmes to help non-financial management understand management accounts.
- Selecting and recruiting finance-department staff at all levels.
- Managing and assessing training and development needs within finance departments.

EDUCATION AND QUALIFICATIONS GAINED
CIMA: Gained 1991
Parkway College of Further Education, BTEC 1987.

Your key skills will always be relevant

There is no need for dates or employer specifics in this section

Education is important if you are returning to work, since it shows concrete achievements

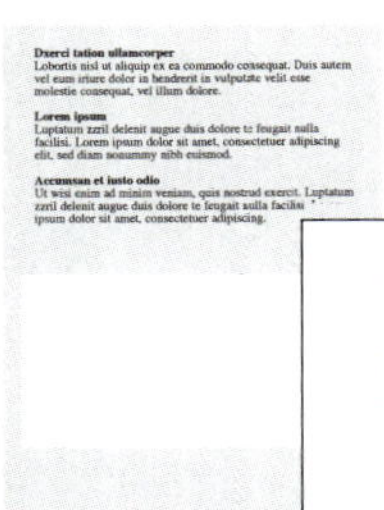

LAST PAGE

Keep details of previous employment brief and relevant, but still focus on achievements

Career Review (contd)

Barker Parts Distribution
Management Accountant 1988–1992
Appointed Divisional Management Accountant on qualification in 1991. Had joined as graduate trainee and was promoted 5 times in 4 years. Gained experience in France and Germany during 9-month secondment.

PERSONAL
Date of birth: 15 July 1966
Married, 2 children
Interests: Badminton, swimming, painting, photography.
References: Available on request.

Your interests may be relevant to an employer

USING YOUR CV EFFECTIVELY

The CV you have spent so long creating now needs to do its job – earn you interviews. In order for it to do that, you must send it with the right covering letter to the right people.

REPLYING TO JOB ADVERTISEMENTS

Job advertisements represent the most open recruitment marketplace. It is a highly competitive field, so your application needs to work hard for you. Careful preparation of a succinct covering letter is every bit as important as the CV itself.

74 Research very thoroughly every organization to which you apply.

Clearly mark any advertisements that look interesting

MATCHING UP

A job advertisement provides only very limited information about the employer and the role. Your challenge is to look behind the actual words, analyze the employer's needs, and match yourself to those criteria. The more precisely your skills can be linked to the job, the greater your chance of being shortlisted – a good guideline is that you should exceed 80 per cent of the advertised requirements.

FOLLOWING INSTRUCTIONS

Read reply instructions carefully. One of the most common reasons for applications being rejected at the first sift is that the reply instructions have not been followed. You will usually be asked to quote a reference number, and may be asked for other information, such as salary progression, or expectations. Only rarely will advertisers come back to you to request information you have omitted – they will have plenty of other applicants who will have followed the instructions.

75 Help your CV to stand out from the rest with a strong covering letter.

CULTURAL DIFFERENCES

In some countries a written, rather than typed, covering letter is expected. In France, in particular, handwritten letters are important as applicants' letters may be sent to a graphologist, who analyzes the handwriting to identify the characteristics of the writer.

DO'S AND DON'TS

- ✔ Do keep dated copies of all the job advertisements that you reply to.
- ✔ Do check if there is a closing date, and reply in plenty of time.
- ✔ Do write a relevant covering letter with every application.
- ✔ Do ensure your application passes the 30-second test.
- ✘ Don't get despondent if you are rejected – accept it and move on to the next application.
- ✘ Don't apply indiscriminately for jobs; each application you make needs to be focused
- ✘ Don't ignore reply instructions.
- ✘ Don't omit specifically requested information.

SURVIVING THE FIRST SIFT

You know that your application may not get more than a 30-second look first time around. Check that you have done the following to ensure it passes that 30-second test and makes it to the next stage:

- You have followed reply instructions;
- Your overall presentation is good;
- Your written style is clear;
- You have been succinct;
- You have shown good attention to detail;
- You have displayed good judgment by selecting the right, relevant information.

76 Limit the number of applications you make each week.

77 Ensure your CV is as relevant as possible.

WRITING THE IDEAL COVERING LETTER

In order to attract the most suitable applicants, job advertisements are very carefully worded. When replying to an advertisement, your covering letter needs to show you have understood the nature of the job being advertised. It must also summarize why your application should receive serious consideration. The letter opposite picks up on all important elements of the job advertisement below and feeds back key phrases. This letter should make it on to the "possible" pile.

78 Include a number of reasons why your application is a strong one.

The job title is the first clue to the nature of any job. The advertisement then clarifies how much experience the employer requires

MATCHING UP ▶

When replying to job advertisements, pick out the key skills and experience that are required for the position and demonstrate how you match them. In this example, the key opposite shows how the applicant gives evidence of his or her suitability for the job – and pays attention to getting the details right.

This company has big plans – it is expanding, so candidates need to be happy in a changing environment

There are a number of responsibilities listed – applicants need a range of skills

Experience in this sector is absolutely vital for this job

General Manager - Training Services (1)

From a zero base 5 years ago, Fountain Training has grown phenomenally and now employs 150 consultants working from 5 offices across the country (5). We intend to continue our aggressive growth programme and plan to open 2 offices overseas in the next 6 months.

We now wish to appoint a General Manger to head up 2 of our existing offices. You will be responsible for the smooth running of these operations (5) whilst also ensuring we continue to grow market share. You will oversee the development of new training services (7) and be responsible for the activities of the sales teams (6).

You will need to have a close understanding of the training market (7) (8) and a record of success in a changing environment (5). Excellent business awareness (8) needs to be supported by a strong business drive and energy (4) to produce results (6). Above all you must be a good general manager and team player (7) with the capacity to manage a growing number of profit centres (10).

If you want to develop your career (9) in the training industry, write to: (2) Chris Williams, Human Resources Director, Fountain Training. Quote ref. no. 18/9DI (1)

79 Sign all your covering letters very clearly.

Key

❶ *Quotes reference number and job title at the start of the letter*

❷ *Uses first name, since he or she (never make assumptions) did in the advertisement*

❸ *Begins with an attention-grabbing opening that shows motivation*

❹ *Shows resourcefulness – this person has initiative and energy*

❺ *Highlights an understanding of the business and its changing demands*

❻ *Illustrates a real achievement in business development – a key skill for this job*

❼ *Underlines the candidate's experience as leader of a successful team*

❽ *Demonstrates real understanding of the advertiser's business*

❾ *Shows personal motivation and a belief in future career possibilities*

❿ *Demonstrates commitment and empathy: "I want to grow with you"*

Chris Williams
Human Resources Director
Fountain Training

❶ General Manager – Training Services: Your ref. 18/9DI

Dear Chris ❷

As an experienced manager in the training industry, your advertisement in the Daily Informer intrigued me ❸. Having read the advertisement closely and conducted a little background research through visiting your Web site ❹, I believe I have a clear understanding of your needs. I hope you will agree my CV warrants closer examination for the following reasons:

❺ I have worked in a high-growth environment for the past 3 years and so am fully aware of the demands this places on operational management.

❻ I am currently responsible for all sales development activities at SKH Associates, the team having exceeded sales targets for the past 2 years.

❼ I led the team, which gained industry accreditation 6 months ago.

❽ Coming from a background as a front-line trainer, I continue to maintain close links with our employer client base and training industry standards bodies.

The role of General Manger would be a natural career progression for me ❾ and I believe that, with your commitment to continued growth, Fountain Training would be an ideal environment in which to develop my career over the longer term ❿.

I would welcome the opportunity of discussing this opportunity further with you.

Yours sincerely

CONTACTING RECRUITMENT COMPANIES

It is employers who pay the recruitment companies' fees – they are not there to give you free advice and support, but to find the right candidate for a particular role. However, they are the gateway to many jobs, and you must know how to deal with them.

80 Take seriously all the feedback recruiters give you about your CV.

81 Make a note of the recruitment applications you make and follow them up.

FINDING A CONTACT

If you plan to contact a recruitment company speculatively, it is prudent to write to a named individual. In some firms this may simply be the person responsible for inputting CVs into databases. However, the best policy is to telephone to find the name of the person who deals with the job area, industry, and/or location in which you are most interested.

IDENTIFYING THE RIGHT RECRUITMENT COMPANY

TYPE OF COMPANY	SERVICE PROVIDED
SEARCH AND SELECTION Handles middle- to senior-management roles in general and specialist fields.	Usually conducts specific search or advertised assignments for each vacancy, but will hold details of prospective candidates on file.
SPECIALIST RECRUITMENT COMPANY Operates in most functional and specialist areas at all levels.	Holds databases of suitably qualified candidates and has a specialist knowledge of a particular industry or profession.
EMPLOYMENT AGENCY Handles vacancies up to first-line management or supervisory level.	Operates on a local basis at the less specialist end of recruitment, although some will have specialist divisions.

THINGS TO DO

1. Use business directories to find appropriate recruitment companies.
2. Use the Internet to find recruitment sites.
3. Scan jobs pages for relevant recruitment agencies.
4. Follow up all unanswered applications.

DECIDING ON YOUR MESSAGE

When writing speculatively, you will be asking to be considered for assignments where your skills and experience are suitable, so be sure to make them clear. In the case of the specialist recruitment companies and employment agencies, your target is an exploratory meeting, where one of their consultants will be able to gain an in-depth appreciation of you. Search and selection firms will tend not to see candidates on a speculative basis, preferring to make appointments only when they are handling a relevant assignment.

GETTING FEEDBACK

If you are rejected at the first stage, you just have to accept that there were better qualified candidates. Occasionally, however, you may feel that you were so close to the specification that you would like some explanation from the recruitment company. Do not question their judgement – ask for constructive feedback about why they rejected you, and how you might better present your case in future.

Keep a note of contacts' names, making sure you have the right spelling

KEEPING RECORDS ▶

Your job search is likely to stretch over several months – good record-keeping of contacts and follow-up communication will make the whole process less stressful.

82 Put the date at the bottom of all the CVs you send out.

FOLLOWING UP

If you have written speculatively to a recruitment company, it is reasonable to expect some sort of response. Ideally, this will be an invitation to meet, but it may just be an undertaking to hold your details on file. If you have heard nothing after about three months, consider contacting them again and sending a fresh copy of your CV.

83 Always write short, clear sentences in your letter and CV.

84 Type letters unless you are specifically asked to write them by hand.

COMPOSING A SPECULATIVE LETTER

Put yourself in the position of the recruiter and remember that they may receive hundreds of speculative letters every week. Try opening your letter with a positive statement. In order to get the reader's attention it can be a good ploy to start with "you" or "your" – for example, "Your company has an impressive reputation in the recruitment of..." or, "You are one of a very few recruitment consultants...". The letter needs to describe the key aspects of your CV succinctly and say why the consultant should be interested in you. You must finally make a clear proposition and leave the reader in no doubt of your career objective.

Hilary Rahman
Accountancy Selection Ltd

Addressing a named individual is very important

Dear Hilary

Your company enjoys an excellent reputation in the recruitment of accountants.

Flattery can be effective, but do not be too gushing – it may come across as insincere

Having built up 5 years' post-qualification experience, I now feel it is time to move on and seek my first Financial Controller role. My CV is attached and I hope you agree that I will make a strong candidate for the following reasons:

- Qualified ACA
- 5 years' post-qualification experience
- 3 years spent in industry role
- Fully mobile, willing to relocate

Bullet points pick out why this person is a strong candidate and summarize their career and present situation

I hope you or your firm may be handling suitable assignments currently or in the near future. I would be very interested to meet with you and discuss any such opportunities.

Having already stated career goals, the letter ends with an invitation for the recruiter to reply

Yours sincerely

▲ **STATING YOUR AIMS**

This is a straightforward letter, written in plain English. It states very clearly the strengths of the candidate and exactly the sort of jobs he or she would like to be considered for.

85 Be confident about demonstrating your industry-specific knowledge.

Use of the correct name, and any title, immediately shows initiative

Letter begins by establishing present status and key achievements

Awkward questions about reasons for looking for a new job are pre-empted

Mr A. Mitchell
Hayward Search Consultants

Dear Mr Mitchell

As Production Director of March Plastics, I have over the past 5 years led a revolution in the manufacture of our core product: disposable cutlery. However, the next phase of this programme is consolidation and so the same level of challenge will not be present. I have therefore decided it is time to look for a move.

As you will see from my CV, I have a wide range of manufacturing experience, and for the past 8 years have operated at Board level. I know from colleagues that you have handled similar positions, and so would like to be considered for any current or future assignments.

My remuneration is a salary package of £70,000 plus the usual executive benefits. I would prefer not to relocate although, as I have commuted weekly for the past 3 years, I would like to be considered for any suitable role anywhere in the country.

I would be happy to meet with you or a colleague to discuss any suitable opportunities.

Yours sincerely

Seniority of the applicant is emphasized

Purpose of the letter is to sell, but the tone is not pushy

Inclusion of current salary indicates desired salary level

Location preference is given, but flexibility is stressed

This is the correct sign-off for a named individual you do not know

86 Beware: specialist recruiters know a lot about your industry and will be aware if you lie or exaggerate.

▲ DEALING WITH HEADHUNTERS

Headhunters are the same as selection companies – but they operate at the top end of the job market, looking for candidates for specific roles. They will not see many applicants on a speculative basis, but a strong letter and CV should mean they will keep your details on file.

CANVASSING EMPLOYERS

Approaching employers "cold" is a highly speculative strategy – you have no idea if they are currently recruiting. However, if you can target the right employers with the right proposition, they may express an interest in meeting you.

87 Include a career summary when making a speculative application.

Be polite to everyone you speak to at a potential new workplace

Use trade magazines to identify potential employers

IDENTIFYING POTENTIAL EMPLOYERS

If you have conducted your career audit and set your career goals, you will be able to identify the employment sectors you would like to work in. A little more research will provide a list of potential employers. Most major employers will include recruitment information on their Web sites, and business directories can also provide useful background information.

DEVELOPING A PROPOSITION

When writing to any employer, you need to decide exactly what you want to do for them – and then tell them precisely. It is no use sending a CV with an "I wondered if you might be interested" message. You need to tell them you want to work as an *abc*, for *def* reasons. You are qualified to do this because of *ghi*, and you want to work for them more than anyone else for *xyz* reasons. Confidence, determination, and flattery are all bound into one. Do not be too pushy, since the chances are they will not be actively recruiting, but express your interest in arranging an exploratory meeting.

MAKING A PROPOSITION TO EMPLOYERS

Tell them what you want to do

↓

Tell them why you want to do it

↓

Tell them why you are qualified to do it

↓

Tell them why you want to do it for them

88 State your goals, but do not limit yourself too much.

89 Keep a note of those employers who do not reply.

DECIDING WHOM TO CONTACT

The right proposition needs to land on the right desk. Personnel or Human Resources departments will be the gatekeepers for current vacancies, but you cannot rely on them forwarding your letter to the right line manager. The best course of action is to identify the right person yourself and write directly to them. If you want to work for the marketing director, write to the marketing director. Be careful not to target too senior a level; you are aiming to see the recipient, and do not want your CV – and you – to be passed down the line.

PROMPTING A RESPONSE

You should receive a polite acknowledgment to any letter you send. However, you cannot always count on it. When writing speculatively, consider saying that you will be making a follow-up call to find out if a meeting would be worthwhile. This demonstrates a positive attitude on your part, and may encourage a response.

90 Show you are motivated, without becoming a nuisance.

QUESTIONS TO ASK YOURSELF

Q Am I using all the routes to a new job that are open to me?

Q Am I sending out the right sort of CV to the right people?

Q Am I giving forms and questionnaires the same kind of detailed attention that I gave to my CV?

Q Should I prepare myself for possible employer tests?

Q Am I coming across as highly motivated?

FILLING OUT FORMS AND QUESTIONNAIRES

Occasionally, an employer may respond with either an application form or a structured questionnaire – either is better than an outright "no". Take some time to read these carefully before starting to complete them. If the form asks you focused, open-ended questions, think about what the employer is trying to find out – for example, are the questions looking for detailed evidence of your transferable skills? Blank sections of forms that ask you to provide "any other information" are a further opportunity for you to sell yourself. Use the analysis of your transferable skills and your career objectives as the basis for your response.

91 Find the name of the person who can give you the job you want.

92 Ensure your career summary is no more than 50 words.

SELLING YOURSELF TO AN EMPLOYER

A sales letter is one of the most difficult business documents to write – and a speculative letter to a potential employer is precisely that. Your research may throw up opportunities, or recent press coverage may provide a lead, and an opening, for communication. Alternatively, start your letter with a powerful statement that headlines your own skills – for example, "Getting customers to pay on time is not easy, but I have spent 10 years doing precisely that". You must then summarize the key elements of your CV and why you want to work for that particular employer. Close with a proposition of what could happen next.

◀ WRITING A LETTER TO A LOCAL EMPLOYER

The recipient of this letter is not necessarily an experienced recruiter, but he will be aware of the needs of his part of the company. This letter states clearly why the applicant should be considered for a specific post.

A degree of formality shows respect for someone the applicant hopes may become their boss

Mr S. Mayne
Financial Controller
Duke Fastenings

Dear Mr Mayne

I drive past Duke Fastenings every morning, and I have heard from an increasing number of acquaintances that you are one of the best employers locally. So I have now plucked up the courage to see if you have a vacancy for a credit control supervisor, or, if you have not, then to ask that you consider me when you do.

A good positive, flattering start

It is unlikely that a job will be available and this sounds a realistic note

As you will see from my CV, I have considerable experience in making sure customers pay on time and have completed courses to gain relevant qualifications.

This shows an understanding of the most important part of the job and goes on to show initiative

I would welcome the opportunity of discussing the matter with you, and to that end I will call your office next week to see if a meeting can be arranged.

It is clear that this is not a half-hearted approach

Yours sincerely

cc. Ms R. Knowles, Personnel Dept

Sending a copy of an application to the personnel department is a courteous thing to do

An opening like this gives all kinds of positive messages. A real interest in your industry also implies a high level of commitment

This strikes the right balance between being enthusiastic and realistic

It is obvious from this bullet-pointed summary that the applicant knows exactly what skills and experience this employer will be looking for

Although pro-active this is still polite and gives the employer a way out if they are not interested

Ms P. Gates
Managing Consultant
PG Human Resources

Dear Ms Gates

Your recent success in winning the New Deal contract made impressive reading in the Human Resources Journal. In the course of my 10 years as an HR professional, I have followed the development of your consulting business and would like to express my interest in joining you, either now or in the not-too-distant future.

As you will see from my CV, I have gained comprehensive experience within HR/Personnel management:

- 5 years generalist HR experience at manager level
- Specialist knowledge of compensation and benefits
- Experience across 3 industry sectors
- Record of success in change-management situations

I would very much like the opportunity to discuss my interest in HR Consulting with you. To that end I will call your office next week to see if an appointment can be arranged.

Yours sincerely

93 Keep copies of every covering letter you send.

94 Avoid using humour in your application – it may be misunderstood.

▲ FOLLOWING LEADS

This letter came about as a result of trade press coverage. Being aware of what is going on in your field will open up possibilities to you and help you to talk confidently at interviews.

DO'S AND DON'TS

- ✔ Do be patient, people you write to may be away or very busy.
- ✔ Do be specific about what you want to do.
- ✔ Do demonstrate your knowledge of a particular company and the industry.
- ✘ Don't be unrealistic, most people you approach will not be recruiting.
- ✘ Don't become despondent if you hear nothing.
- ✘ Don't become a nuisance.

USING THE INTERNET

The Internet is the fastest-growing recruitment medium, and e-mail is increasingly used in all areas of recruitment. The Internet offers access to jobs worldwide. However, because it is such a huge resource, the career seeker needs to use it selectively.

95 Be careful using e-mail for sending confidential information.

96 Use a spell-checker to detect spelling mistakes when e-mailing applications.

CHANGING PRACTICES

Although the Internet may be rewriting the way business is conducted in a number of fields, in recruitment the basic rules remain the same. Your next job will still come through a job advertisement, personal networking, or through your details being on a database. However, the Internet changes the way companies operate and gives you greater access and more opportunities to network.

LOOKING FOR JOBS ON THE INTERNET

TYPE OF SITE	HOW TO USE THE SITE
THE JOB SITE Job sites come in all shapes and sizes, specialist and non-specialist. Some are simply noticeboards.	The big recruitment sites will have thousands of vacancies across entire countries or continents. Begin by limiting your search by location and type of vacancy. Many have search engines to help you refine your search.
THE CORPORATE SITE These are specific to one company and are used as a promotional tool that may include current vacancies.	Increasingly, companies of all sizes are establishing Web sites. These sites are a good source of background information on a company. They may advertise vacancies, and you may be invited to leave your details at the site.
THE DATABASE SITE These are run by the large Internet-based recruiting companies. This type of site is on the increase.	At these sites you will be invited to complete extensive on-line questionnaires that build a profile of your skills, which are then matched against employers' needs. You should also receive feedback on your profile.

USING E-MAIL EFFECTIVELY

E-mail may be a great boon for its speed and simplicity, but be careful how you use it. Most e-mail systems allow you to request a receipt to be sent back to you when an item is delivered, or opened and read. Since a job application is an important document, this is a sensible precaution, and because it is an automatic function, it requires no effort on the part of the recipient. Use the e-mail itself as a covering letter – this remains the first thing a potential employer will see, so make sure that you take as much care writing this part of your document as you would if you were posting your job application.

USING INTERNET RECRUITMENT SITES

Select the sites most relevant to your job search

↓

Register your details with them

↓

Revisit each site regularly to check on any developments

↓

Update your details every three months

Check you have attached the correct documents before sending your e-mail

MAILING CVS ELECTRONICALLY

The safest way to send your CV is as an attachment to your e-mail message – make sure you know which word-processing packages can be opened by the recipient. There are also some different conventions in page layout – the most obvious is in the United States, where Quarto, rather than A4, is the standard set up. Above all, avoid sending your CV as a text only e-mail – your application will look just the same as all the others.

POSTING CVS ON THE WEB

For those people who are able to conduct a very public career search, there is the option of making a CV available on their own Internet site and posting details within various search engines. For most people, taking advantage of this option will require specialist instruction – nevertheless, it represents the ultimate in self-promotion.

97 Make sure a Web CV accurately reflects who you are.

KEEPING UP YOUR JOB SEARCH

For most people, a career search will last many months. You must be methodical throughout and weather both good news and bad. The whole process will take up a lot of time, but it will be an experience from which you will learn a lot about yourself.

98 If re-contacting, check your original contact is still working there.

KEEPING A DIARY

From the day you send your first job application, start keeping a job-search diary. Record what you sent to whom and when, and keep copies of job advertisements and covering letters. Having all this information at hand will enable you to keep track of responses received, as well as whom to chase. The diary will also help you to judge if it is time to make contact again, especially if you have received no reply.

Keeps a record of who has been contacted and when in a job-search diary

99 Try not to take the rejections you receive personally.

100 Prepare very thoroughly for all your interviews.

COPING WITH REJECTION

Every time you send a job application, you set expectations within yourself. However, more often than not you will have to cope with having those expectations dashed. The reality is that, no matter how suitably qualified you may be, there will be many others equally well qualified. Of all the qualities needed by the job searcher, persistence is the most important. The break you are looking for is that your CV obtains you a meeting. Every time that happens, you can celebrate a small victory.

RE-CONTACTING PEOPLE

Events move quickly for employers and recruitment companies, and memories are short. Using your diary, you will be able to monitor whom you have contacted and when, and what response you received. You may consider contacting a different individual on a second attempt, or, if you received a moderately warm response the first time, a mildly updated CV can be sent after two or three months. Contacting the same organization every week is excessive, but a phone call every three months or so may increase your chances of success.

101 Celebrate every time your CV earns you an interview.

Prompted by job-search diary, phones to ask about progress of application

Remains positive throughout application process and at interviews

Receives some rejection letters

USING YOUR CV AS A DEVELOPMENT TOOL

Even when you have completed your career search and landed a new job, make sure you review your CV regularly. Set aside time twice a year to bring it up to date, identifying recent achievements, and any changes to your role. A well-kept CV tells you how your career is progressing and helps to identify any areas that you should be developing. It will also make the start of your next career search easier.

ASSESSING YOUR SKILLS

This very simple questionnaire will help you to gain a better idea of what you think your skills profile might be. The most important part of this exercise is to discover the relationship between what you see as your strengths and your weaknesses. You must be honest with yourself; try to use 1 or 4 and only score 2 or 3 where you are in doubt. Your scores from this questionnaire will be used for the analysis of your profile on pages 68–69. The profile you produce may suggest new avenues for you to explore.

OPTIONS

1 Disagree
2 Slightly disagree
3 Slightly agree
4 Agree

1 I am a good motivator and enjoy empowering others to achieve goals.

1 2 3 4

2 I thoroughly plan and schedule my time as well as the tasks I work on.

1 2 3 4

3 I am meticulous in my approach and try to ensure quality standards are met.

1 2 3 4

4 I gain the co-operation of other people because they are convinced by my arguments.

1 2 3 4

5 I am proficient in all the technical skills required in my chosen career.

1 2 3 4

6 I analyze issues thoroughly so that I can solve problems easily.

1 2 3 4

7
I speak confidently and clearly to both individuals and larger groups.

1 2 3 4

8
I write clearly and have been praised for my ability to communicate on paper.

1 2 3 4

9
I am driven by commercial principles and achieving best value.

1 2 3 4

10
I am often ingenious in my approach and question traditional working methods.

1 2 3 4

11
I will often initiate projects and am always ready to make a decision.

1 2 3 4

12
I understand the wider implications and the longer-term impact of decisions.

1 2 3 4

13
I am sensitive to the needs of other people and work well with colleagues.

1 2 3 4

14
I adapt well to changing situations and respond quickly to changing needs.

1 2 3 4

15
I am stable under pressure and remain calm in the face of setbacks.

1 2 3 4

16
I work hard because I am committed to furthering my own career.

1 2 3 4

ANALYZING YOUR PROFILE

By plotting out your responses to the questionnaire on the previous pages, you will gain a clear picture of your transferable skills. This will enable you to emphasize your strengths and play down – or overcome – your weaknesses.

CREATING YOUR PROFILE

To create your profile, photocopy the chart opposite or draw one up. Mark a cross between the numbers 1 and 4 in the first column according to your answers to the 16 questions on pages 66–67, then draw a line joining the crosses. Look at the line; where it falls to the left it indicates your weaker tendencies, where it falls to the right it shows your stronger ones. In preparing your CV, focus on your strengths, since it is these that will get you your next job. By gaining a better understanding of your skills, you can gauge how best they will work for you. You will also need to account for your weaknesses.

▼ ASSESSING SKILLS

Your completed chart will give you a clear indication of where your strengths and weaknesses lie. It can also help you make the most of your skills and deal with any areas that you feel need to be improved.

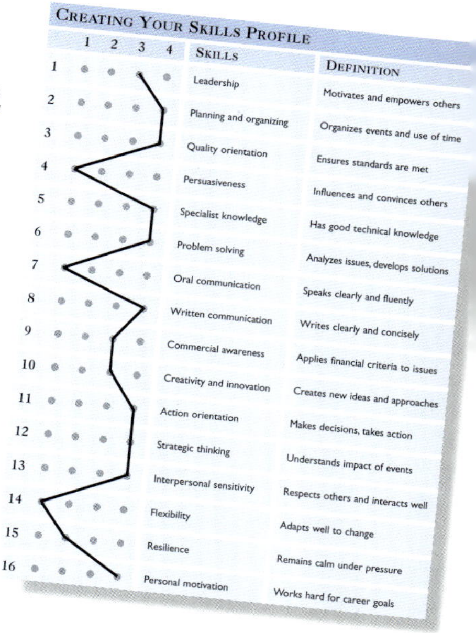

UNDERSTANDING YOUR WEAKNESSES

There are two ways of dealing with your weaknesses: you can either live with them or you can overcome them. Your approach will depend on whether the skills are integral to the work you may be taking on. The likelihood is that a number of your perceived weaknesses are in areas in which a possible lack of expertise will not adversely affect your prospects, or they may indicate a dislike for some particular tasks. Those things that you do not enjoy and are not good at are probably best avoided. The skills that you do need to fulfil your career ambitions need to be tackled through formal training or personal development. If it will improve your chances of success, enrol in a course or spend time reading self-help books that cover the skills you need.

Creating Your Skills Profile

	1	2	3	4	Skill(s)	Definition
1	●	●	●	●	Leadership	Motivating and empowering others
2	●	●	●	●	Planning and organizing	Organizing events and using time
3	●	●	●	●	Quality orientation	Ensuring standards are met
4	●	●	●	●	Persuasiveness	Influencing and convincing others
5	●	●	●	●	Technical competence	Possessing the required job skills
6	●	●	●	●	Problem-solving	Analyzing issues, finding solutions
7	●	●	●	●	Oral communication	Speaking clearly and fluently
8	●	●	●	●	Written communication	Writing clearly and concisely
9	●	●	●	●	Commercial awareness	Applying financial criteria to issues
10	●	●	●	●	Creativity and innovation	Originating ideas and approaches
11	●	●	●	●	Action orientation	Making decisions, taking action
12	●	●	●	●	Strategic thinking	Understanding the impact of events
13	●	●	●	●	Interpersonal sensitivity	Respecting others, interacting well
14	●	●	●	●	Flexibility	Adapting well to change
15	●	●	●	●	Resilience	Remaining calm under pressure
16	●	●	●	●	Personal motivation	Working hard for career goals

PSYCHOMETRIC TESTING

One of the fairest means of assessing a candidate's ability is by psychometric testing. Understanding and practising the basic types of test will enable you to improve your skills and performance.

UNDERSTANDING TESTS

Psychometric tests come in many forms. The purpose of each kind of test is to assess your ability in a specific skill area or to gain an understanding of your personality in relation to the work environment. As with all tests, it is essential to be prepared.

102 Use your skills profile to help you identify your career strengths.

POINTS TO REMEMBER

- Tests form only part of an employer's overall assessment of your abilities.
- A good test performance is important, but a high test score alone will not win you the job.
- The more questions you answer correctly, the higher your test score will be.
- Pychometric tests can teach you a great deal about your strengths and weaknesses.

COMPARING CANDIDATES

In a psychometric test, all candidates answer the same standard questions, so each candidate's results are directly comparable to those of the other candidates who have taken the test. Since everyone is different, and different jobs require various standards of ability, your results will be compared with the performance of a similar group (known as the norm, or comparison, group). In this way employers are able to make an objective assessment of your abilities that is not dependent on, and cannot be influenced by, either the tester or the interviewer.

PERSONALITY QUESTIONNAIRES

You may sometimes be asked to complete a personality questionnaire as part of the selection process for a job. As the name suggests, this is not an ability test, but a series of questions that identifies your main personality attributes, preferences, style, and your relevant transferable skills.

ASSESSING YOUR SKILLS

When used and administered correctly, tests help an employer to find the right person for a particular job. An employer will first profile the needs of the job, noting the type and level of skills required, and will then select tests to help identify these skills in candidates. The test results give a detailed profile of the abilities of each candidate. Tests are also used to identify the training requirements of employees so that individual development programmes can be tailored to meet the employer's own needs. The aim of psychometric tests is to help employers make fairer, and therefore better, decisions about people.

IDENTIFYING THE PRINCIPAL TYPES OF ABILITY TEST

TYPE OF TEST	AIMS OF TEST
VERBAL REASONING	To assess your ability to understand and evaluate written information, including documents, correspondence, reports, and letters.
CHECKING AND ACCURACY	To gauge how accurately you are able to check information, whether working with computers, stocks, orders, tables, or accounts.
NUMERICAL REASONING	To evaluate your ability to understand facts and figures and draw appropriate conclusions from them by analyzing numerical data presented in tables, graphs, and diagrams.
SPATIAL REASONING	To assess your ability in visualizing how three-dimensional objects look when presented as two-dimensional drawings. This is important for work involving plans or designs.
DIAGRAMMATIC REASONING	To test your ability to recognize rules or patterns within logical sequences and apply them to problems. This type of test is often used in technical disciplines.

PREPARING FOR TESTS

By practising for psychometric tests you will increase your confidence and gain a better idea of what to expect at a testing session. Use the practice tests provided on pages 74–81 to familiarize yourself with the types of questions you may have to answer.

103 Find out what kinds of tests you will be asked to complete.

USING PRACTICE TESTS

As with real tests, the practice tests on pages 74–81 come with full instructions. Real tests are timed, so these practice tests also give time guidelines. Try to keep to these guidelines, since they will give you an idea of the pace required; the secret is to work as quickly and accurately as you can. Most real tests have example questions that you can attempt before you begin, but using the practice tests on the following pages will help you to prepare before the test day.

104 Check the time allowed for each test before you begin working.

Look for useful practice material in a variety of sources, including newspapers and magazines

◀ **IMPROVING YOUR SKILLS**
Take every opportunity to improve your verbal and numerical skills. Reading a wide variety of material will sharpen your analytical skills and keep your mind active. A few minutes spent doing this each day will soon pay dividends.

COMPLETING THE TESTS

When attempting the practice tests, find a quiet room where you will not be interrupted and where you can work comfortably at a desk or table. Make sure you have all the equipment you require. Photocopy the tests before you start, or work in pencil so you can re-use the tests. You will need a rubber, paper for rough working, and a watch with a second hand or an accurate timer. You may practice the numerical tests with or without a calculator – for some tests you will be allowed to use one. Do not start until you are sure you understand the instructions. Failure to understand instructions is the most common cause of candidates performing below their ability level.

105 Maintain a positive attitude throughout a testing session.

106 Mark your best guess if you are not sure of one of the answers.

PREPARING FOR A TESTING SESSION

Ask the company to send you sample tests of the type you will be taking

↓

Practice taking the tests and note any questions you want to ask

↓

Arrive at the test session in plenty of time

↓

During the test work confidently and with complete concentration

DEVELOPING YOUR SKILLS

Prepare for testing sessions by giving your brain some mental exercise. For verbal tests read newspapers, reports, and business journals and do some verbal problem-solving exercises, such as crosswords. If you will be taking numerical tests, study tables of data and practise your mental arithmetic. For diagrammatic tests try logic-based problems. In all cases, buying a puzzle book and working on a range of problems will exercise your mind and help you perform to the best of your ability in a real test.

DO'S AND DON'TS

- ✔ Do work as quickly and accurately as you possibly can.
- ✔ Do exactly as you are told.
- ✔ Do read each question thoroughly before attempting it.
- ✘ Don't worry if you can't complete all of the questions.
- ✘ Don't waste time on difficult questions.
- ✘ Don't assume that all tests are put together in the same way.

TEST 1: VERBAL REASONING

In this test there are two passages, followed by a number of statements. Evaluate the statements in the light of the information or opinions contained in the passage, and select your answer according to the rules below:

- *Fill in Circle A if the statement is patently TRUE, or follows logically, given the information or opinions contained in the passage.*
- *Fill in Circle B if the statement is patently UNTRUE, or the opposite follows logically, given the information or opinions contained in the passage.*
- *Fill in Circle C if you CANNOT SAY whether the statement is true or untrue or follows logically without further information.*

See how many you can complete in 3 minutes.

ANSWER SHEET

1	Ⓐ	Ⓑ	Ⓒ
2	Ⓐ	Ⓑ	Ⓒ
3	Ⓐ	Ⓑ	Ⓒ
4	Ⓐ	Ⓑ	Ⓒ
5	Ⓐ	Ⓑ	Ⓒ
6	Ⓐ	Ⓑ	Ⓒ

The big economic difference between nuclear and fossil-fuelled power stations is that nuclear reactors are more expensive to build and decommission, but cheaper to run. So disputes over the relative efficiency of the two systems revolve not just around the prices of coal and uranium today and tomorrow, but also around the way in which future income should be compared with current income.

1 The main difference between nuclear and fossil-fuelled power stations is an economic one.

2 The price of coal is not relevant to discussions about the relative efficiency of nuclear reactors.

3 If nuclear reactors were cheaper to build and decommission, they would have the economic advantage.

At any given moment we are being bombarded by physical and psychological stimuli competing for our attention. Although our eyes are capable of handling more than 5 million bits of data per second, our brains are capable of interpreting only about 500 bits per second. With similar disparities between each of the other senses and the brain, it is easy to see that we must select the visual, auditory, or tactile stimuli that we wish to compute at any specific time.

4 Physical stimuli are usually successful in the competition for our attention.

5 The capacity of the human brain is sufficient to interpret nearly all of the stimuli the senses can register.

6 Our eyes are able to cope with a greater input of information than our ears.

TEST 2: CHECKING AND ACCURACY

In this test you are provided with two lists of reference numbers. The list on the left is the original draft, and the list on the right is the final version. Look for any differences (errors) that occur between the two lists. Fill in the appropriate circle on the answer sheet for any column where you find a difference. If there are NO differences (errors) in a line, fill in circle "E" on your answer sheet. There can be more than one error in any given line, so you may have to mark more than one letter on your answer sheet for each line.

See how many you can check in 2 minutes.

ANSWER SHEET					
1	Ⓐ	Ⓑ	Ⓒ	Ⓓ	Ⓔ
2	Ⓐ	Ⓑ	Ⓒ	Ⓓ	Ⓔ
3	Ⓐ	Ⓑ	Ⓒ	Ⓓ	Ⓔ
4	Ⓐ	Ⓑ	Ⓒ	Ⓓ	Ⓔ
5	Ⓐ	Ⓑ	Ⓒ	Ⓓ	Ⓔ
6	Ⓐ	Ⓑ	Ⓒ	Ⓓ	Ⓔ
7	Ⓐ	Ⓑ	Ⓒ	Ⓓ	Ⓔ
8	Ⓐ	Ⓑ	Ⓒ	Ⓓ	Ⓔ
9	Ⓐ	Ⓑ	Ⓒ	Ⓓ	Ⓔ
10	Ⓐ	Ⓑ	Ⓒ	Ⓓ	Ⓔ

	A	B	C	D		A	B	C	D
1	12	KT	3D	47-98		22	KT	3D	47–98
2	91	PM	C5	62-64		91	PM	C5	62–64
3	3	AJ	B4	L55-57		3	JA	B4	L51–55
4	17	AM	S5	B7-22		18	PM	S5	B7–12
5	11	ZZ	PO	M9-10		11	ZZ	PO	M9–10
6	89	SR	X8	F14-16		98	XR	Y9	F14–16
7	34	XX	K7	35-38		34	YY	K7	35–39
8	87	KP	M6	A12-13		87	M6	KP	A12–13
9	7	JZ	K2	H8-9		7	JZ	K2	H8–9
10	69	JI	S5	K66-69		96	IJ	5S	K64–66

TEST 3: INTERPRETING DATA

In this test, use the facts and figures in the statistical tables below to answer the questions opposite. Only one of the options is correct in each case. Question 2 has ten options, so if you select an option from AB–BC you will have to fill in more than one circle. You may try this test with or without a calculator.

See how many you can complete in 4 minutes.

ANSWER SHEET

1	Ⓐ	Ⓑ	Ⓒ	Ⓓ	Ⓔ
2	Ⓐ	Ⓑ	Ⓒ	Ⓓ	Ⓔ
3	Ⓐ	Ⓑ	Ⓒ	Ⓓ	Ⓔ
4	Ⓐ	Ⓑ	Ⓒ	Ⓓ	Ⓔ
5	Ⓐ	Ⓑ	Ⓒ	Ⓓ	Ⓔ
6	Ⓐ	Ⓑ	Ⓒ	Ⓓ	Ⓔ

Population Structure 1985

	Population at start of year (millions)	Live Births per 1000 population (Jan–Dec)	Deaths per 1000 population (Jan–Dec)	Percentage of population at start of year aged under 15	60 or over
UK	56.6	13.3	11.8	19	21
France	55.2	13.9	10.0	21	19
Italy	57.1	10.1	9.5	19	19
West Germany	61.0	9.6	11.5	15	20
Spain	38.6	12.1	7.7	23	17

Production of 15mm Buttons, July–December

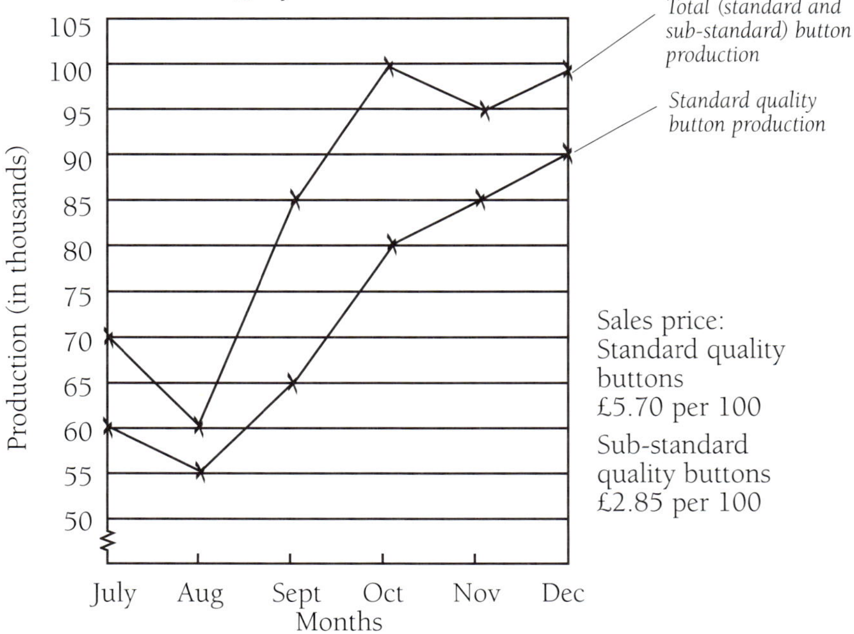

Sales price:
Standard quality buttons
£5.70 per 100

Sub-standard quality buttons
£2.85 per 100

1 Which country had the highest number of people aged 60 or over at the start of 1985?

A	B	C	D	E
UK	France	Italy	W. Germany	Spain

2 What percentage of the total 15mm-button production was sub-standard in September?

A	B	C	D	E
10.5%	13%	15%	17.5%	20%
AB	AC	AD	AE	BC
23.5%	25%	27.5%	28%	30.5%

3 How many live births occurred in 1985 in Spain and Italy together (to the nearest 1000)?

A	B	C	D	E
104,000	840,000	1,044,000	8,400,000	10,440,000

4 What was the net effect on the UK population of the live birth and death rates in 1985 ?

A	B	C	D	E
Decrease of 66,700	Increase of 84,900	Increase of 85,270	Increase of 752,780	Cannot say

5 By how much did the total sales value of November's button production vary from October's?

A	B	C	D	E
£28.50 (Decrease)	£142.50 (Decrease)	£285.00 (Increase)	£427.50 (Decrease)	No change

6 What was the loss in potential sales revenue attributable to the production of sub-standard (as opposed to standard) buttons over the six-month period?

A	B	C	D	E
£213.75	£427.50	£2,137.50	£2,280.00	£4,275.00

TEST 4: NUMERICAL REASONING

Choose the correct answer from the five options given for each question below and fill in the corresponding circle on the answer sheet. You may use a calculator to help you if you wish. Use the table provided for questions 6 and 7.

See how many you can complete in 7 minutes.

1 If a maintenance contract costs £87 per month and a technician call-out not under a contract costs £325, how many call-outs per year would make the contract worthwhile?

A	B	C	D	E
4	5	6	7	8

2 If every 250 bottles of bleach require 16.25 litres of solvent to produce, how much solvent is required to produce 6,500 bottles of bleach?

A	B	C	D	E
42.3 litres	100.0 litres	121.9 litres	422.5 litres	1,219.0 litres

3 Last year's sales target was £265,000. This year's target is £328,000. By what percentage has this year's sales target increased over last year's?

A	B	C	D	E
17%	29%	43%	81%	none of these

4 A total of 5,200 analyses required 17,300 hours of computer time. Approximately how much time would be required to perform an additional 300 analyses if all other factors remain unchanged?

A	B	C	D	E
330 hours	540 hours	660 hours	940 hours	1,000 hours

5 A batch of shampoo requires 510 litres of herbal extracts and 13,400 litres of water. What is the approximate ratio of water to herbal extracts?

A	B	C	D	E
26:1	3.8:1	1:26	1:38	1:260

ANSWER SHEET

1	Ⓐ	Ⓑ	Ⓒ	Ⓓ	Ⓔ
2	Ⓐ	Ⓑ	Ⓒ	Ⓓ	Ⓔ
3	Ⓐ	Ⓑ	Ⓒ	Ⓓ	Ⓔ
4	Ⓐ	Ⓑ	Ⓒ	Ⓓ	Ⓔ
5	Ⓐ	Ⓑ	Ⓒ	Ⓓ	Ⓔ
6	Ⓐ	Ⓑ	Ⓒ	Ⓓ	Ⓔ
7	Ⓐ	Ⓑ	Ⓒ	Ⓓ	Ⓔ
8	Ⓐ	Ⓑ	Ⓒ	Ⓓ	Ⓔ
9	Ⓐ	Ⓑ	Ⓒ	Ⓓ	Ⓔ
10	Ⓐ	Ⓑ	Ⓒ	Ⓓ	Ⓔ
11	Ⓐ	Ⓑ	Ⓒ	Ⓓ	Ⓔ
12	Ⓐ	Ⓑ	Ⓒ	Ⓓ	Ⓔ

	Profit Year 1	Year 2	Year 3
Branch A	£4.6m	£4.8m	£4.7m
B	£2.8m	£2.9m	£2.5m
C	£6.1m	£6.4m	£6.6m

6 How many times over the three-year period did A, B, and C experience a reduction in profit?

A	B	C	D	E
0	1	2	3	4

7 By what percentage did the total profit made by A, B, and C increase from Year 1 to Year 3?

A	B	C	D	E
2.%	2.2%	20%	22%	102.%

8 Temporary staff are paid £6.00 per hour. If 47 hours were worked last week by each of seven temporary staff, what was the total bill?

A	B	C	D	E
£197	£282	£329	£846	£1,974

9 If 625kg of fruit are required to produce 200 jars of jam, approximately how much fruit is required to produce 450 jars of jam?

A	B	C	D	E
144kg	531kg	864kg	1,270kg	1,406kg

10 A survey carried out on 1,500 people showed that 37% liked a new product, while 32% were indifferent. If the rest said they disliked the product, how many people were in this category?

A	B	C	D	E
48	237	465	945	1,020

11 In an average week, the computer is down for 2.75 hours. Lost revenue per hour is £425,000. What is the approximate total revenue lost in a 52-week year?

A	B	C	D	E
£0.23m	£8.04m	£12.10m	£47.26m	£60.78m

12 The operating profit last year was £7.75m. If there is an increase this year of 13%, what will this year's operating profit be?

A	B	C	D	E
£7,945,000	£8,126,800	£8,346,200	£8,757,500	none of these

TEST 5: SPATIAL REASONING

In this test, you are given a pattern that, if cut out, could be folded to make a three-dimensional shape (a box). Decide which, if any, of the boxes in the sequences below could be made by folding the pattern, and fill in the appropriate circle on the answer sheet. If none of the boxes could be made from the pattern, fill in circle "E" on the answer sheet.

See how many you can complete in 3 minutes.

ANSWER SHEET

1	Ⓐ	Ⓑ	Ⓒ	Ⓓ	Ⓔ
2	Ⓐ	Ⓑ	Ⓒ	Ⓓ	Ⓔ
3	Ⓐ	Ⓑ	Ⓒ	Ⓓ	Ⓔ
4	Ⓐ	Ⓑ	Ⓒ	Ⓓ	Ⓔ

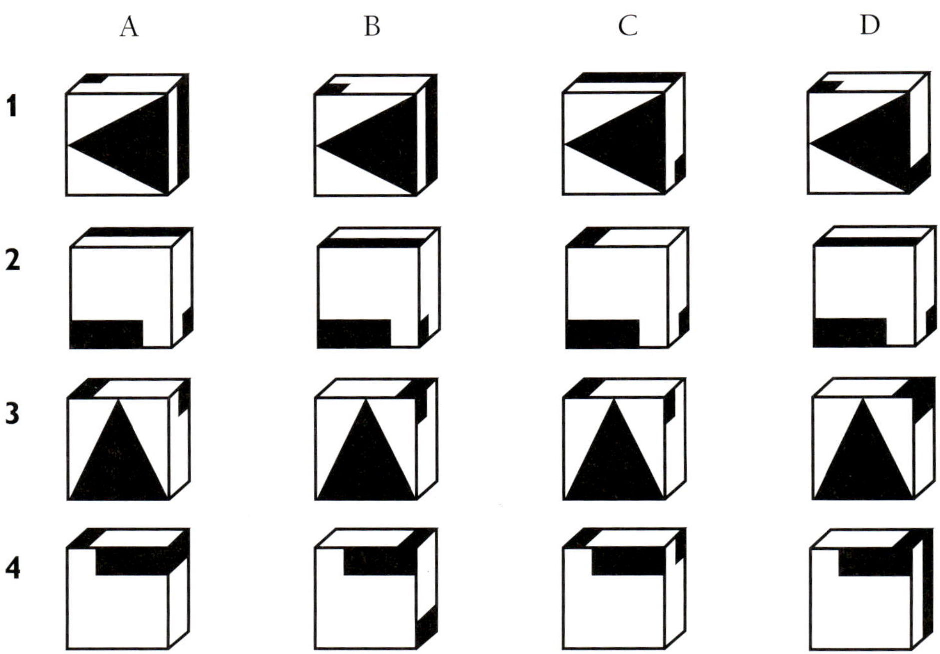

TEST 6: DIAGRAMMATIC REASONING

This test consists of a series of diagrams which follow a logical sequence. Choose the next diagram in the series from the five options on the right. Indicate your answer by filling in the appropriate circle on the answer sheet.

See how many you can complete in 3 minutes.

ANSWER SHEET

1	Ⓐ	Ⓑ	Ⓒ	Ⓓ	Ⓔ
2	Ⓐ	Ⓑ	Ⓒ	Ⓓ	Ⓔ
3	Ⓐ	Ⓑ	Ⓒ	Ⓓ	Ⓔ
4	Ⓐ	Ⓑ	Ⓒ	Ⓓ	Ⓔ
5	Ⓐ	Ⓑ	Ⓒ	Ⓓ	Ⓔ
6	Ⓐ	Ⓑ	Ⓒ	Ⓓ	Ⓔ

1

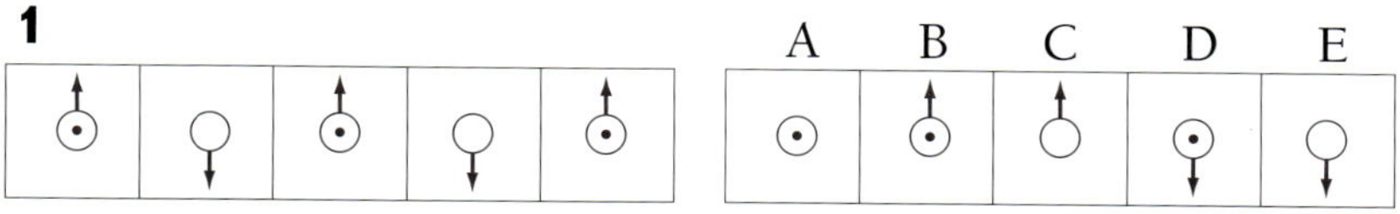

2

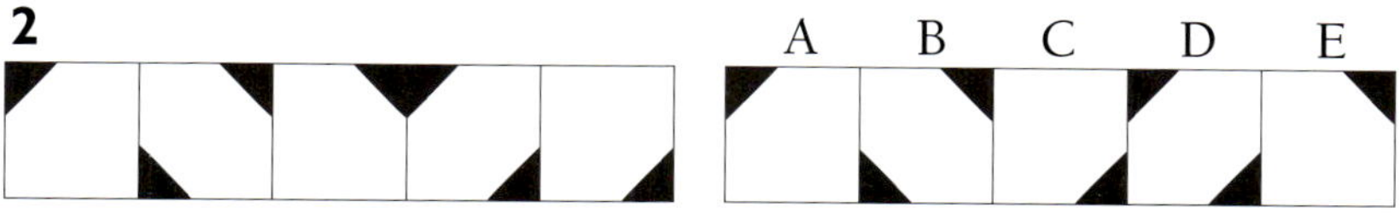

3

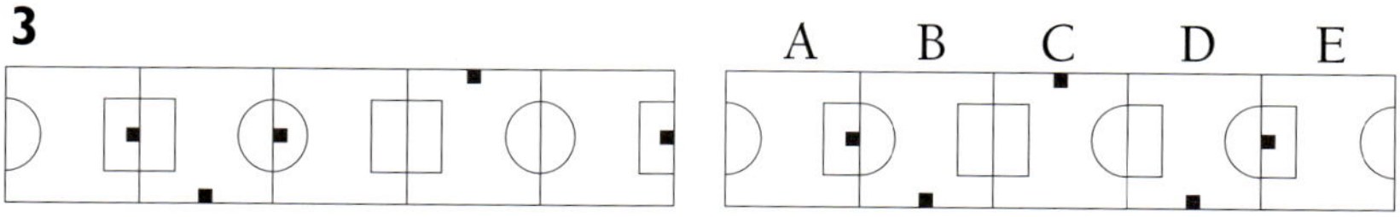

4

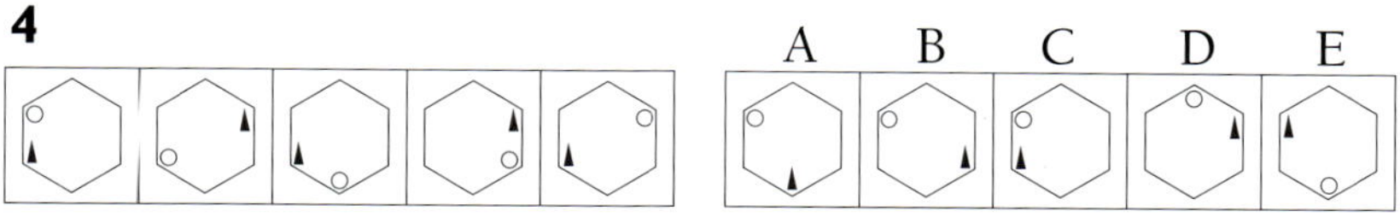

5

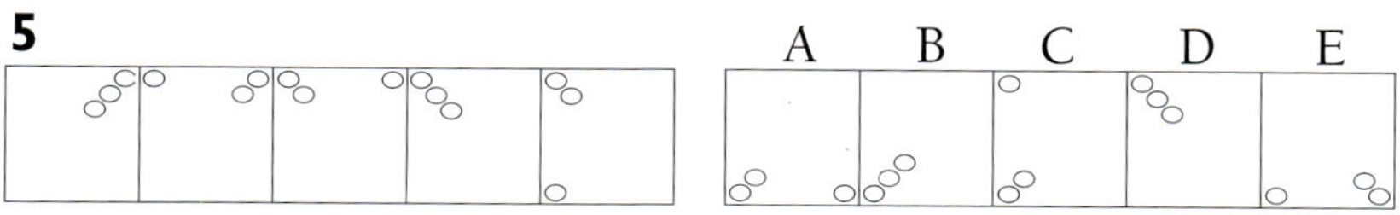

6

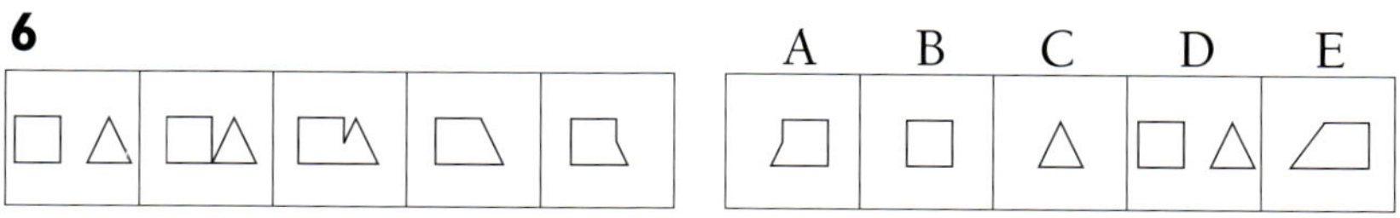

EVALUATING YOUR RESULTS

Opposite you will find the answers to the practice tests on pages 74–81. Take some time to work out where you did well and where you did not. Having had some practice, you will now have a better idea of what to expect at a real testing session.

107 If you use glasses or a hearing aid, remember to bring them to the test.

POINTS TO REMEMBER

- It is rare to achieve full marks. A typical score is half to three quarters of the maximum score.
- Very few people attempt all questions on every test.
- Very few people answer all of the questions they attempt correctly.
- If you answered many questions but got many answers wrong, work more slowly next time.
- If you got most of your answers right but did not complete all questions within the time allowed, work more quickly.

SCORING THE TESTS

Check your answers against the tables opposite. When assessing your results, remember that these tests are individual assessments of your abilities and that candidates do not pass or fail a psychometric test. In a real test situation, you are most likely to be given a "percentile" score. To be told you achieved "60th percentile" does not mean that you scored 60%, but that you scored better than 60% of a group of people similar to yourself who have taken the test.

108 Have a good night's sleep before a testing session.

After a testing session, ask for feedback on your performance to help you assess your strengths and weaknesses

GETTING FEEDBACK ▶
Potential employers should be willing to discuss your test performance. This is still an interview situation, so present yourself in a professional manner.

ANSWER TABLES

Test 1 (page 74) VERBAL REASONING

1	Ⓐ	Ⓑ	●
2	Ⓐ	●	Ⓒ
3	●	Ⓑ	Ⓒ
4	Ⓐ	Ⓑ	●
5	Ⓐ	●	Ⓒ
6	Ⓐ	Ⓑ	●

Test 3 (pages 76–77) INTERPRETING DATA

1	Ⓐ	Ⓑ	Ⓒ	●	Ⓔ
2	●	●	Ⓒ	Ⓓ	Ⓔ
3	Ⓐ	Ⓑ	●	Ⓓ	Ⓔ
4	Ⓐ	●	Ⓒ	Ⓓ	Ⓔ
5	Ⓐ	Ⓑ	Ⓒ	Ⓓ	●
6	Ⓐ	Ⓑ	●	Ⓓ	Ⓔ

Test 5 (page 80) SPATIAL REASONING

1	Ⓐ	●	Ⓒ	Ⓓ	Ⓔ
2	Ⓐ	Ⓑ	Ⓒ	●	Ⓔ
3	Ⓐ	Ⓑ	●	Ⓓ	Ⓔ
4	Ⓐ	Ⓑ	Ⓒ	Ⓓ	●

Test 2 (page 75) CHECKING AND ACCURACY

1	●	Ⓑ	Ⓒ	Ⓓ	Ⓔ
2	Ⓐ	Ⓑ	Ⓒ	Ⓓ	●
3	Ⓐ	●	Ⓒ	●	Ⓔ
4	●	●	Ⓒ	●	Ⓔ
5	Ⓐ	Ⓑ	Ⓒ	Ⓓ	●
6	●	●	●	Ⓓ	Ⓔ
7	Ⓐ	●	Ⓒ	●	Ⓔ
8	Ⓐ	●	●	Ⓓ	Ⓔ
9	Ⓐ	Ⓑ	Ⓒ	Ⓓ	●
10	●	●	●	●	Ⓔ

Test 4 (pages 78–79) NUMERICAL REASONING

1	●	Ⓑ	Ⓒ	Ⓓ	Ⓔ
2	Ⓐ	Ⓑ	Ⓒ	●	Ⓔ
3	Ⓐ	Ⓑ	Ⓒ	Ⓓ	●
4	Ⓐ	Ⓑ	Ⓒ	Ⓓ	●
5	●	Ⓑ	Ⓒ	Ⓓ	Ⓔ
6	Ⓐ	Ⓑ	●	Ⓓ	Ⓔ
7	Ⓐ	●	Ⓒ	Ⓓ	Ⓔ
8	Ⓐ	Ⓑ	Ⓒ	Ⓓ	●
9	Ⓐ	Ⓑ	Ⓒ	Ⓓ	●
10	Ⓐ	Ⓑ	●	Ⓓ	Ⓔ
11	Ⓐ	Ⓑ	Ⓒ	Ⓓ	●
12	Ⓐ	Ⓑ	Ⓒ	●	Ⓔ

Test 6 (page 81) DIAGRAMMATIC REASONING

1	Ⓐ	Ⓑ	Ⓒ	Ⓓ	●
2	Ⓐ	●	Ⓒ	Ⓓ	Ⓔ
3	Ⓐ	Ⓑ	Ⓒ	●	Ⓔ
4	Ⓐ	Ⓑ	Ⓒ	●	Ⓔ
5	Ⓐ	Ⓑ	●	Ⓓ	Ⓔ
6	Ⓐ	●	Ⓒ	Ⓓ	Ⓔ

JOB-SEEKER'S DIRECTORY

Knowing where to look for job vacancies is one of the most important weapons in the job-seeker's armoury. Use a variety of sources to give yourself the best possible chance of success.

MEDIA

Newspapers and magazines provide sources of job vacancies that are easily accessible and relatively inexpensive. Trade publications carry advertisements that are specific to their particular field and contain useful background information, while newspapers offer a more general range.

TRADE PRESS

Publications that deal with a specific career area offer focused sources of job vacancies. This section of the directory lists a selection of useful magazines and journals, providing website details only when the website offers job vacancies.

CONSTRUCTION

Architects Journal (Weekly) Tel: 020 8956 3100; www.emap.com/construct
EDITORIAL PROFILE: Covers all aspects of architecture from high-profile international projects to issues concerning small local practices.
JOBS ADVERTISED: CAD technicians, architects, property buyers, secretarial, interior designers.

New Civil Engineer (Weekly) Tel: 020 7505 6619; www.careersinconstruction.com
EDITORIAL PROFILE: Covers issues such as legislation and construction news.
JOBS ADVERTISED: Engineering vacancies – civil, environmental and design, project managers, contracts managers.

EDUCATION

Times Educational Supplement, The (Weekly) Tel: 01708 378379; www.tes.co.uk
EDITORIAL PROFILE: News-led, with some features and a comprehensive job section.
JOBS ADVERTISED: Various teaching, primary and secondary, all subjects.

Times Higher Educational Supplement, The (Weekly) Tel: 020 7782 3000
EDITORIAL PROFILE: News and analysis related to higher education.
JOBS ADVERTISED: Teaching posts across UK higher education establishments.

ENGINEERING

Chemical Engineer, The (Fortnightly) Tel: 01788 578214; www.icheme.org
EDITORIAL PROFILE: Aimed at chemical and process engineers and managers. It has news, features, and opinion related to the industry, from oil to food and drink.
JOBS ADVERTISED: Project management, consultancy and engineering, process, sales, and lectureships.

Engineer, The (Weekly)
EDITORIAL PROFILE: Covers a range of engineering issues. Aimed at those employed in the engineering manufacturing industry.
JOBS ADVERTISED: Design, production, electronics, mechanical engineering.

Structural Engineer, The (Fortnightly) www.istructe.org.uk
EDITORIAL PROFILE: Provides members with world-wide news and information on practice, design, development, and research in structural engineering.
JOBS ADVERTISED: Structural, project, and chartered engineers, technicians.

Surveyor (Weekly) Tel: 020 7973 6400
EDITORIAL PROFILE: Aimed at professionals in local government. Covers highways, transportation waste management, and water, as well as contemporary specialist features such as air quality and pollution.
JOBS ADVERTISED: Highway engineering, highway technicians, and inspectorate positions – a range of jobs in the local government sector.

FINANCE AND ACCOUNTANCY

Accountancy (Monthly) Tel: 020 7920 8878; www.accountancymag.co.uk
EDITORIAL PROFILE: Institute Journal covering all business, technical, and professional aspects of accountancy, and relevant broad-spectrum articles.
JOBS ADVERTISED: Large recruitment section for all levels of accountants plus financial consultants, analysts, auditors, and managers.

Accountancy Age (Weekly)
EDITORIAL PROFILE: Newspaper for qualified accountants.
JOBS ADVERTISED: Financial accountants, financial directors, vacancies at all levels.

INFORMATION TECHNOLOGY

Computer Weekly (Weekly) Tel: 01444 475613; www.computerweekly.co.uk

EDITORIAL PROFILE: One of the two largest general IT papers. High-quality editorial and a busy recruitment section. More programming jobs than *Computing*.

JOBS ADVERTISED: IT positions at all levels, a good consultancy section.

Computing (Weekly) Tel: 020 7316 9000; www.computingnet.co.uk

EDITORIAL PROFILE: One of the two largest general IT papers. Perceived as carrying more management jobs than *Computer Weekly*.

JOBS ADVERTISED: Covers all aspects of IT with a busy senior appointments section.

INSURANCE

Insurance Age (Monthly) Tel: 020 7505 8000; www.insuranceage.com

EDITORIAL PROFILE: Includes articles on aspects of insurance, latest news and product updates, as well as predictions and trends for insurance professionals.

JOBS ADVERTISED: Clerical, sales.

Insurance Times (Weekly) Tel: 01509 233100

EDITORIAL PROFILE: Includes news, and product and technology updates.

JOBS ADVERTISED: Covers the whole range of vacancies in the insurance industry.

LAW

Law Society's Gazette (Weekly) Tel: 01235 465656; www.lawsoc.org.uk

EDITORIAL PROFILE: Authoritative source of information on Law Society activities and policies, and an independent observer of the law and the legal profession.

JOBS ADVERTISED: Comprehensive range of appointments for solicitors across the UK.

Lawyer, The (Weekly) Tel: 020 7970 2789; www.the-lawyer.co.uk

EDITORIAL PROFILE: Circulated mainly among commercial law firms, *The Lawyer* features high-quality editorial content.

JOBS ADVERTISED: Commercial lawyers, partnerships, legal support roles.

Legal Business (Monthly) Tel: 020 7396 9313; www.legalease.co.uk

EDITORIAL PROFILE: Aimed at senior commercial lawyers.

JOBS ADVERTISED: Top legal positions covering all commercial areas. Mainly agency advertisements but some client-paid.

MANAGEMENT AND HR

People Management (Weekly) Tel: 01483 733 864

EDITORIAL PROFILE: Aimed at professionals in personnel, training, and development.

JOBS ADVERTISED: Extensive range, including employee relations officers, training managers, staff development managers, and area personnel officers.

Personnel Today (Fortnightly) Tel: 01444 475604

EDITORIAL PROFILE: Covers industry news, analysis, opinion, and in-depth features.

JOBS ADVERTISED: Includes top-level personnel appointments, plus general human resources personnel, managers, personnel officer training and development, advisers, and IT.

MARKETING AND MEDIA

Campaign (Weekly) Tel: 020 8845 8545

EDITORIAL PROFILE: Includes advertising campaign news and reviews.

JOBS ADVERTISED: Managerial and executive marketing.

Design Week (Weekly) Tel: 020 7970 6666

EDITORIAL PROFILE: The leading title in the graphic art and design industry.

JOBS ADVERTISED: Graphic artists, designers, and managers for positions within the industry and with end-users.

Marketing (Weekly) Tel: 020 8845 8545; www.marketing.haynet.com

EDITORIAL PROFILE: Includes marketing, retailing, media news, in-depth articles.

JOBS ADVERTISED: Marketing vacancies at all levels, including a considerable number of brand-management positions.

Marketing Week (Weekly) Tel: 020 7439 4222; www.mad.co.uk/mw/

EDITORIAL PROFILE: Aimed at marketing decision-makers. Includes news about marketing, media, advertising, and promotion.

JOBS ADVERTISED: Marketing vacancies at all levels – managerial, brand, product account directors, market research, direct marketing.

PR Week (Weekly) Tel: 020 8503 0588

EDITORIAL PROFILE: Includes news, analysis, and articles.

JOBS ADVERTISED: Press officers, public relations vacancies – executive, managerial, publicity officers, and co-ordinators.

MEDICINE

BMJ – British Medical Journal (Weekly) Tel: 020 7383 6270

EDITORIAL PROFILE: The official journal of the BMA. Mostly research papers but also includes news and some editorial features.

JOBS ADVERTISED: Classified journal pullout contains specialist posts, locum placements, overseas jobs. Separate pullouts for GP and clinical research posts.

British Dental Journal (Fortnightly) Tel: 01256 329242

EDITORIAL PROFILE: Includes ideas, opinions, developments, and key issues in dentistry – clinical, practical, and scientific.

JOBS ADVERTISED: Mainly dentist, some hygienist, and nursing vacancies.

Lancet, The (Weekly) Tel: 020 7436 4981; www.thelancet.com
EDITORIAL PROFILE: Includes clinical information, reports, some editorial features.
JOBS ADVERTISED: Full- and part-time appointments in many areas of medicine.

Nursing Standard (Weekly) Tel: 020 8423 1066; www.nursing-standard.co.uk
EDITORIAL PROFILE: Affiliated to the RCN, contains political and clinical information for nurses, midwives, and health professionals.
JOBS ADVERTISED: Nurses.

Nursing Times (Weekly) Tel: 020 7874 0200
EDITORIAL PROFILE: Promotes itself as the independent voice of nursing, the main recruitment channel for nursing.
JOBS ADVERTISED: Nurses, midwives, educators, researchers.

Pharmaceutical Journal (Weekly) Tel: 01491 829272
EDITORIAL PROFILE: The main source of pharmaceutical career and job information.
JOBS ADVERTISED: Researchers, advisors.

Veterinary Record, The (Weekly) Tel: 020 7240 2032
EDITORIAL PROFILE: Research, papers, and articles on developments in veterinary medicine.
JOBS ADVERTISED: Veterinary surgeons, nurses, assistants, full and part-time.

RESEARCH AND DEVELOPMENT

Nature (Weekly) Tel: 020 7843 4985; www.nature.com
EDITORIAL PROFILE: Covers news, views, correspondence, and scientific and educational reviews, along with the latest technology.
JOBS ADVERTISED: Post-doctoral research positions across a wide range of disciplines, plus a good selection of directorships and senior scientist positions.

New Scientist (Weekly) Tel: 01444 475636; www.newscientist.com
EDITORIAL PROFILE: Features reports of scientific advancement and interest.
JOBS ADVERTISED: Research assistants, technicians, experimental officers, lecturers.

RETAIL

Drapers Record (Weekly) Tel: 020 7520 1500
EDITORIAL PROFILE: The primary fashion business magazine. Covers all aspects of women's wear and the shoe industry.
JOBS ADVERTISED: Shop floor to managing directors.

Grocer, The (Weekly) Tel: 01293 610255; www.foodanddrink.co.uk
EDITORIAL PROFILE: Covers all aspects of grocery retailing, includes industry and product news, latest promotions, food and health issues.
JOBS ADVERTISED: Senior, executive, retail management, and sales appointments.

NEWSPAPERS

Listed below are some of the most important job sections in major daily newspapers. This is not a complete list of sources, and it is worth looking in the national and regional press for vacancies in all fields.

ARTS AND MEDIA

Daily Telegraph (Saturday) Broadsheet, www.appointments-plus.com
The Guardian (Monday) Broadsheet, www.jobsunlimited.co.uk
Independent (Tuesday) Broadsheet

EDUCATION

Daily Telegraph (Wednesday) Broadsheet, www.appointments-plus.com
The Guardian (Tuesday) Broadsheet, www.jobsunlimited.co.uk

ENGINEERING

Express (Thursday) Tabloid

FINANCE AND ACCOUNTANCY

Daily Mail (Thursday) Tabloid
Financial Times (Monday, Wednesday, Thursday) Broadsheet, www.ft.com
Independent (Wednesday) Broadsheet

INFORMATION AND TECHNOLOGY

The Guardian (Thursday) Broadsheet, www.jobsunlimited.co.uk
Independent (Monday) Broadsheet
Daily Mail (Tuesday) Tabloid
Financial Times (Wednesday) Broadsheet, www.ft.com

LAW

The Times (Tuesday) Broadsheet

PUBLIC SECTOR

The Guardian (Wednesday) Broadsheet, www.jobsunlimited.co.uk

SALES

Express (Thursday) Tabloid

SECRETARIAL AND ADMINISTRATION

Independent (Wednesday) Broadsheet
The Times (Wednesday) Broadsheet

SENIOR APPOINTMENTS

Daily Telegraph (Thursday) Broadsheet, www.appointments-plus.com
The Times (Thursday) Broadsheet
Independent (Thursday) Broadsheet
The Sunday Times Broadsheet

RECRUITMENT AGENCIES

Agencies are concentrated in the most lucrative industries. Vacancies handled by recruitment agencies vary depending on the client base each one serves; for example, a City branch of a financial recruitment agency will handle more banking vacancies than a regional branch of the same agency. The following selection is intended as a starting point.

ADMINISTRATIVE AND SECRETARIAL

Adecco (150 branches) Tel: 020 8207 5000; www.adecco.co.uk
Elstree Way, Borehamwood, Hertfordshire WD6 1HY

Blue Arrow (100 branches) Tel: 01727 853891
Churchill House, 26 Upper Malborough Street, St. Albans AL1 3UU

Brook Street (120 branches) Tel: 01727 84829; www.brookstreet.com
Clarence House, 134 Hatfield Road, St. Albans, Hertfordshire AL1 3UU

Kelly Services (100 branches) Tel: 020 7247 4494
Rodwell House, 100 Middlesex Street, London E1 7HD

Manpower (220 branches) Tel: 020 7224 6688; www.manpower.co.uk
International House, 66 Chiltern Way, London W1M 1PR

Office Angels (113 branches) Tel: 020 8741 4000; www.office-angels.co.uk
3 Shortland, Hammersmith, London W6 8RR

Pertemps (120 branches) Tel: 01676 525 000
Meridan Hall, Main Road, Meridan, Warwickshire CV7 7PT

Reed Employment Services (132 branches) Tel: 020 8399 5221; www.reed.co.uk
Tolworth Tower, Tolworth, Middlesex KT6 7DN

CONSTRUCTION

Anders Glaser & Wills Tel: 020 8882 0172; www.cdi-agw.demon.co.uk
288 Chase Road, Southgate, London N14 6HF

Berisford Blake Thomas Tel: 020 7828 1555; www.bbt.co.uk
59 Buckingham Gate, London SW1E 6AJ

Eden Brown Recruitment Ltd (2 branches) Tel: 020 7309 1300; www.edenbrown.co.uk
17–29 Sun Street, London EC2M 2PT

Euroelite Tel: 020 7256 5555; www.euroelite.co.uk
69 Broad Street, London, EC2M 1NQ

Hays Montrose Tel: 0800 716026; Fax: 020 7233 7296;
www.hays-montrose.com
Hays Montrose House, 1 Wilton Street, London SW1V 1AB
Hill McGlynn Tel: 020 7240 4433; www.hillmcglynn.com
6 Henrietta Street, Covent Garden, London WC2E 8PS
Resource Management Tel: 020 7700 2424
189 Holloway Road, London N7 8DJ

ENGINEERING

Agencies dealing with engineers tend to be specialized, having strong links with local employers. Access them through the specialist business press.

FINANCE AND ACCOUNTANCY

ABPM (5 branches) Tel: 0114 252 6900; Fax: 0114 252 6901
6 President Buildings, Saville Street East, Sheffield, South Yorks S4 7UQ
Accountancy Additions (2 branches) Tel: 020 7247 6414; Fax: 020 7377 9884
Devonshire House, 146 Bishopsgate, London EC2M 4JX
Badenoch & Clark (9 branches) Tel: 020 7583 0073; Fax: 020 7353 3908;
www.badenochandclark.com
16–18 New Bridge Street, London EC4V 6HU
FSS Financial (3 branches) Tel: 020 7209 1000; www.fss.co.uk
Charlotte House, 14 Windmill Street, London W1P 2DY
Harrison Willis Tel: 020 7806 6700; www.hw-group.com
52–54 High Holborn, London WC1V 6RL
Hays Accountancy Personnel (10 branches) Tel: 020 7638 3955; Fax: 020 7920 0432; www.hays-ap.co.uk
141 Moorgate, London EC2M 6TX
Hays Banking Personnel Tel: 020 7515 2266; Fax: 020 7531 1521
Parker House, Admirals Way, London E14 9UQ
HW Group Plc (8 branches) Tel: 020 7240 2101; www.hwgroup.com
Cardinal House, 114 St. Martins Lane, London WC2N 4AZ
Michael Page City and Finance Tel: 020 7831 2000; Fax: 020 7831 2612;
www.michaelpage.net
Page House, 39–41 Parker Street, London WC2B 5LH
Robert Half (16 branches) Tel: 020 7395 9600; www.roberthalf.co.uk
Walter House, Bedford Street, 418 The Strand, London WC2R 0PT
Robert Walters Tel: 0207 379 3333; www.robertwalters.com
10 Bedford Street, London WC2E 9HE

INFORMATION TECHNOLOGY

Best People Ltd (6 branches) Tel: 020 7300 9000; www.best-people.co.uk
1 Bedford Avenue, London WC1B 3AS

Computer Futures (12 branches) Tel: 020 7458 7755; www.compfutures.com
3rd Floor, 17 St. Helen's Place, London EC3A 6DE

Computer People (9 branches) Tel: 020 7440 2000; www.computerpeople.co.uk
Picadilly House, 33 Lower Regent Street, London SW1Y 4NB

Elan Computing Ltd (7 branches) Tel: 020 7830 1332; www.elan.co.uk
Elan House, 5–11 Fetter Lane, London EC4A 1QX

Harvey Nash Plc (2 branches) Tel: 020 7333 0033; www.taps.com/harvey-nash
13 Bruton Street, London W1X 7AH

Hays IT (10 branches) Tel: 01525 222222; Fax: 01525 229289; www.hays-it.co.uk
The Tythe Barn, High Street, Edlesborough, Dunstable LU6 2HS

Monarch Recruitment Ltd (2 branches) Tel: 0870 603 9072; Fax: 0870 603 9077;
www.monarchrecruitment.co.uk
1st Floor, 279 Farnham Road, Slough, Berks SL2 1HB

Progressive Computer Recruitment Ltd (2 branches) Tel: 020 8971 8888;
www.progressive.co.uk
St. George's House, 5 St. George's Road, London SW19 4DR

Spring IT Personnel (7 branches) Tel: 0121 788 6600; www.spring.com/itper
Spring House, The Crescent, Solihull Parkway, Birmingham Business Park, B37 7YE

INSURANCE

Hays Inter-Selection (10 branches) Tel: 020 7480 7220; Fax: 020 7481 9888;
www.hays-interselection.com
Roman Wall House, 1–2 Crutched Friars, London EC3N 2HT

Insurance Personnel (3 branches) Tel: 020 8680 4044; Fax: 020 8680 5055
Howard House, The Arcade, 32–34 High Street, Croydon, Surrey CR0 1YB

Insurance Recruitment Group, The Tel: 020 7929 2500; Fax: 020 7929 2100
24 Lime Street, London EC3M 7HS

Reed Insurance Personnel (10 branches) Tel: 020 7621 0733; Fax: 020 7621 0235
37–39 Lime Street, London EC3M 7AY

LAW

Anakin Seal Ltd (4 branches) Tel: 020 7477 6522; www.anakinseal.com
120 Old Bond Street, London EC2N 1AR

HW Daniels Bates Legal (2 branches) Tel: 020 7806 6700; www.hwgroup.com
High Holborn House, 52–54 High Holborn, London WC1V 6RL

Quarry Dougall Recruitment Tel: 020 7405 6062; www.qdgroup.com
37–41 Bedford Row, London WC1R 4JH
Reynell Legal Recruitment Tel: 020 7439 5881; Fax: 020 7439 5882
20 Soho Square, London W1A 1DS
ZMB (2 branches) Tel: 020 7523 3725; Fax: 020 7523 3726; www.zmb.co.uk
37 Sun Street, London EC2M 2PL

MEDICAL

BNA/Medic International (160 branches) Tel: 01707 267 030
The Colonnades, Beaconsfield Close, Hatfield, Herts AL10 8YD
Medacs (5 branches) Tel: 0800 442 200; www.medacs.com
The Old Surgery, 49 Otley Street, Skipton, North Yorkshire BD23 1BR
PRN Recruitment (3 branches) Tel: 020 8558 9466; Fax: 020 8558 2682
Kirkdale House, Kirkdale, London E11 1HP
Professional Healthcare Services (4 branches) Tel: 01924 378 870
20 Queen Street, Wakefield, West Yorks WF1 1JR
Smile Paramedic and Locum Group (2 branches) Tel: 020 7407 6579
20 Borough High Street, London SE1 9QG

RESEARCH AND DEVELOPMENT

Kelly Scientific Resources Tel: 020 8810 0123; www.kellyscientific.com
32–34 The Broadway, Ealing, London W5 2NP
Lab Staff Tel: 01753 542 738; www.labstaff.co.uk
Buckland House, Waterside Drive, Langley Business Park, Slough SL3 6EZ

SALES

Alexander Chapel Associates (3 branches) Tel: 0117 985 9986;
6 Berkley Square, Clifton, Bristol BS8 1HG
ATA Selection (9 branches) Tel: 0117 944 4600; Fax: 0117 942 5584
Portland House, 22–24 Portland Square, Bristol BS2 8RZ
Austin Benn Consultants Ltd (3 branches) Tel: 01628 788554
Ground Floor, Sierra House, St. Mary's Walk, Maidenhead, Berks S16 1OJ
Michael Page Sales and Marketing (4 branches) Tel: 020 7831 2000
www.michaelpage.net
Savannah House, 11 Charles II Street, London SW1Y 4QZ
SRS (4 branches) Tel: 020 7831 5980; Fax: 020 7839 5231
Savannah House, 11 Charles II Street, London SW1Y 4QZ

INDEX

ACKNOWLEDGMENTS

AUTHOR'S ACKNOWLEDGMENTS

This book has very much been a team effort: I would like to thank Fiona Jobson and Geoff Thiel for their support, interest, and guidance. I enjoyed working with the team at Dorling Kindersley and would single out Gwen Edmonds and Laura Watson for their (almost) daily input and Stephanie Jackson for thinking of me in the first place. I would also like to thank SHL Group plc for permission to use their Inventory of Management Competencies, which was used as the basis for all references to transferable skills, and the Psychometric Tests.

PUBLISHER'S ACKNOWLEDGMENTS

The table of transferable skills on p.17, based on the SHL Inventory of Management Competencies, and the Psychometric Tests on pages 74–81 are reproduced by kind permission of SHL Group plc, who retain all rights in those works.

Information included in the Job-Seeker's Directory is reproduced from "Choices Candidate Yearbook" by kind permission of Career Counsel, who retain all rights in the text.

Dorling Kindersley would like to thank the following for their help and participation:

Editorial Michael Downey, Nicola Munro, Jane Simmonds, David Tombesi-Walton, Sylvia Tombesi-Walton; **Design** Austin Barlow, Jamie Hanson, **DTP assistance** Rob Campbell; **Indexer** Hilary Bird; **Photography** Steve Gorton; **Photographer's assistant** Nici Harper.

Models Philip Argent, Marian Broderick, Angela Cameron, Kuo Kang Chen, Patrick Dobbs, Carole Evans, Richard Hill, James Kearns, Maggie Mant, Frankie Mayers, Sotiris Melioumis, Mutsumi Niwa, Kiran Shah, Lois Sharland, Lynne Staff, Gilbert Wu, Wendy Yun; **Make-up** Karen Fundall.

Special thanks to the following for their help throughout the series:
Ron and Chris at Clark Davis & Co. Ltd for stationery and furniture supplies; Pam Bennett and the staff at Jones Bootmakers, Covent Garden, for the loan of footwear; Alan Pfaff and the staff at Moss Bros, Covent Garden, for the loan of the men's suits; David Bailey for his help and time; Graham Preston and the staff at Staverton for their time and space.

Suppliers Apple Computer UK Ltd., Austin Reed, Church & Co., Compaq, David Clulow Opticians, Elonex, Escada, Filofax, Gateway 2000, Mucci Bags.

Picture researcher Andy Sansom; **Picture librarians** Rachel Hilford, Charlotte Oster.

PICTURE CREDITS

The publisher would like to thank the following for their kind permission to reproduce their photographs:

Key: *b*=bottom; *c*=centre; *l*=left; *r*=right; *t*=top
PowerStock Photolibrary/Zefa: 31*bl*; **The Stock Market**: Jose L. Pelaez Inc 7*r*
Tony Stone Images: Bruce Ayres 4*c*; **Telegraph Colour Library**: D. Avuk 25*tr*; Masterfile 31*cl*.
Front cover **Tony Stone Images**: Bruce Ayres *c*.

AUTHOR'S BIOGRAPHY

Simon Howard is a leading authority on recruitment. He has led a number of recruitment companies and been a director of the SHL Group, a leader in the design and publishing of psychometric tests. As well as writing the "Jobfile" column for the *Sunday Times*, he contributes regularly to *People Management* and has written on recruitment issues for BBC Television.